SMARTPHONE LINK

PRO TREK Connected

After installing the PRO TREK Connected app on your phone, you can link with the watch and automatically adjust its time setting.

Phone linking simplifies a number of operations, including FISH MEMO record management, quick access to the current time in 300 cities around the globe, and time setting configuration.

⊃ FISHING POINT SETTING

After you have downloaded the App you can specify any one of approximately 3,300 points at ports around the world. Simply select a port on a map to access Best Fishing Times, Tide Graph information, Moon data, and sunrise and sunset times for that location.

SMART WATCH

T0362737

PRT-B70-1D

PRT-B70-2D

PRT-B70-5D

FISHING GUIDE TO
WESTERN PORT

WESTERN ENTRANCE • BALNARRING
STONY POINT & COWES • UPPER WESTERN PORT
CORINELLA • EASTERN ENTRANCE • PHILLIP ISLAND
KILCUNDA TO CAPE PATERSON

Consultants – Fishing Maps:
Paul Worsteling

Cartography:
Australian Fishing Network

Illustrations:
Geoff Wilson

ACKNOWLEDGEMENTS

Dedication
I dedicate this book to my beautiful wife Cristy and my little boy Jet Reef. You are both the greatest things that ever happened to me, and the only two things on this planet that I love more than separating fish from water.
And to my parents Hans and Henny. Thank you for getting me off to a fine start in life. I hope I make you proud.

Thank you
I would like to thank every angler and friend who has helped with the information in this book. No one man has all the answers and it is the unnamed people who unselfishly gave information that make this, such a great publication. One man who requires special thanks is Colin Guilmartin. His help in the Eastern Entrance area of the Port was priceless. Thank you all so much for sharing your knowledge so that others will benefit.

DISCLAIMER
The publisher and authors except no responsibility or liability with respect to the accuracy or otherwise of maps, GPS marks and other advice.
Such information is merely an aid to locating fishing marks and a guide to the area and under no circumstances to be used in place of admiralty charts for boating navigation. Common sense and a healthy respect for the weather, tides and sea conditions should be combined to make your outing on Western Port both rewarding and safe.

Published and distributed by
AFN Fishing & Outdoors
PO Box 544, Croydon, Victoria 3136
Telephone: (03) 9729 8788
Email: sales@afn.com.au
Website: www.afn.com.au

First published by Sportfish Australia Publications 2000
Totally revised and updated 2007
Updated 2010
Updated 2015
Updated 2022

ISBN: 9781 8752 2817 1

Printed in China

FOREWORD

By Merv Hughes

Paul Worsteling has made a serious impact in fishing circles since starting in a part time job in the sporting section at Kmart, at age 14. He soon got a job at the local tackle store (Cranbourne Fishing Tackle) and purchased it at age 22 after working part time at the store while completing a secondary physical education and health teaching degree at Rusden Teachers College. After four years at uni, Paul taught for just three days before choosing fishing as a full time profession. His media exploits began with talks at local angling clubs and community radio after he landed an AAA Australian record 275 kilo mako shark off Phillip Island on 12 kilo line. He was soon writing for fishing magazines including *Fishing World, Modern Fishing, South East Fishing, Sportsfishing* and *Bluewater.*

Paul got his big break with a co-hosting role on the Rex Hunt Fishing Adventures television program on Channel Seven. He held that position for four years. When the show finished the popular IFISH program was born. IFISH is seen around Australia on Network 10 and overseas in dozens of countries on pay television.

Due to his line of work, Paul has fished in some of the most amazing areas on the planet, but he started fishing on Western Port over 20 years ago and it still holds a very special place in his heart.

After jetting around the world for weeks on end fishing, you will find him on Western Port on his day off, with his wife Cristy, his boy Jet and his dog Otto, by his side.

Paul has been lucky enough to meet tens of thousands of anglers through his Cranbourne Tackleworld and Berwick ShimanoWorld fishing stores. Every one of them has taught him something about fishing over the years, and he is keen to pass that information on. After reading this book, Paul believes that you will never go fishing on Western Port with the 'hope' of catching a fish again. Instead, you will be secure with the knowledge that you probably will catch a fish...it is only the species, size and quantity that may vary.

I have fished with Paul on several occasions. We caught plenty and had lots of good laughs. I hope reading his book will give you a similar result.

LEGEND FOR MAPS

MAP KEY

——————— Road

——————— Highway/Main Road

 Boat Ramp

 Beacon

 Excellent Fishing

 Starboard Buoy/Light

 Port Buoy/Light

○ Warning Buoy/Light

64 GPS Mark

 Marine Sanctuary

 Rocks

 Hill

FISH SPECIES KEY

1. Snapper

2. Whiting

3. Australian salmon

4. Gummy shark

5. Snook

6. Elephant shark

7. Trevally

8. Mullet

9. Mulloway

10. Calamari

11. Thresher

12. Garfish

13. Gunard

14. School shark

DEPTH IN METRES

Sand/Mud Flats

0–6 m

6–12 m

12–20 m

20–40 m

Over 40 m

CONTENTS

Western Port is an amazing waterway that supports a wide variety of species, some that are residents and others on their seasonal migration.

The author with a quality Western Port snapper. Fish like this are not uncommon year round.

CHAPTER 1
FINDING FISH IN WESTERN PORT

*'The good thing about Western Port is that you can always find a fish somewhere,
and you can always find somewhere to fish.'*

Phillip Islands coastline is rugged but offers some amazing fishing both inside Western Port and offshore in Bass Strait.

Western Port is a genuine first class fishery that has inspired me towards angling success for many decades. During the early stages, the fishing bug was bled into me with some of the Port's most highly prized species notched into my belt.

It is certainly an interesting waterway and is the most consistent producer of some of the largest saltwater species caught in Victoria.

With its arterial-like expanse of small channels that weave their way around, it is a tough waterway to understand, that is unless you spend countless hours on the water trying to figure it all out.

The Port has a total area of around 680 square kilometres, 270 of which are exposed at low tide and it is at low tide when you'll first want to explore it.

There are only two types of skippers on Western Port. Those that have run a ground, and those who are going to. Unbeknown to many new comers to the Port, on a high tide, you'd think you can drive anywhere. Well that is until you're high a dry on the first mud bank you attempt to cross that's coved by less than a foot of water.

Western Port is a very daunting location if you don't have a thorough understanding of the tides and shallow sand/mud banks. This is why driving around the Port on a low tide is a great introduction, helping to give you a good insight as to its basic layout.

Despite its reputation, when it comes to fishing it is impressive to say the least. Mulloway, flathead, Australian salmon, cowanyoung, mackerel, tailor, garfish, flounder, bream, estuary perch, red mullet, sweep, leather jackets, zebra fish, snotty trevalla, trevally, ling, cod, pike, snook, shark (both pelagic and bottom dwelling), mullet, stargazers and barracouta to mention a few, are all fish that can be caught here.

A thorough under-standing of the area will also enable anglers to lock horns with Western Port's big 'two'. The famous King George whiting, which pull hard and taste sweet and of course big red snapper in excess of 14 kilos (30 pounds).

Gummy sharks to thirty kilos use Western Port as a breeding ground over the spring as it offers an ideal location to throw their pups and they love the deep channels through the winter months. March sees the start of the annual elephant fish invasion and captures of big mulloway are becoming a regular occurrence rather than a mistake.

Western Port is con-sidered a safe port by most anglers due to the protection and shelter offered by French Island and provided you are aware of the tides and impending weather condi-tions, a fishing outing on Western Port can be most rewarding.

Fishing success on Western Port will only come when the angler has a thorough understanding of the tide and its movement patterns. Understanding the Western Port tides, is more than just knowing the highs and lows—it is an in-depth science that must be mastered in order to catch fish. Anglers who take the time to fully understand the tides and how they affect the species they intend to target will find success with much greater ease. Even since the first book on Western Port, I have learnt so much about the tides and how to fish them for best results, and I am keen to pass this information on.

With over twenty years experience fishing on the Port and around the world I have attempted to answer, with the aid of reasonably accurate maps, almost every query on Western Port, particularly in reference to specific fish species, how to catch them and most importantly, where to find them. I also understand that not every angler owns a boat. With this in mind, I have paid particular attention to land based locations around the Port and the surf and rock fishing hotspots from Phillip Island through to Cape Patterson.

As an avid game fisherman, I have also taken the time to highlight the potential for Victorian game fishing in Bass Strait for shark species such as makos, blues, threshers, seven gills and whalers. As the holder of several AAA Australian shark Records including a 275 kilo mako taken off Woolamai and a 75 kilo thresher taken off Kilcunda, I feel qualified to point you in the right direction.

I hope you thoroughly enjoy this read and most importantly, that it sees you catching more fish on our beautiful Western Port. I have been fortunate enough to fish in some of the most stunning places in the world, but I still call Western Port home and long for its beauty and fishing diversity no matter where I find myself fishing on this amazing planet.

FINDING FISH

As with real estate, the rule with fishing is simple in that the three most important factors are LOCATION, LOCATION and LOCATION. Take the worst angler you know to the trout farm and they are almost guaranteed to clean up, yet if you take the best angler you know to a barren dam they are certain to draw a blank. This analogy stresses the importance of location in fishing success. It doesn't matter how good you are or how much knowledge and experience you have, if you are not in the right spot, you may be wasting your time. Due to this simple fact, the importance of the correct hot spot cannot be highlighted enough. For this reason I have pushed the main focus of this publication towards the 'where to fish' aspect. Each area of the Port has been broken up into sections with corresponding maps and GPS marks. These maps however, are only intended as an aid to locating fishing marks and should not be used in place of Admiralty charts for boat navigation. Fortunately, it seems that every second boat these days has a full chart plotter, which makes navigating a dream. For around a $1000 you can get a full colour Lowrance fish finder/depth sounder/mapping GPS unit and I strongly recommend it. The safety aspect alone makes it worth its weight in gold and with fuel prices continually on the rise you will pay it off in no time with direct routes between any two points assured.

GPS marks mentioned throughout the text are merely to assist locating landmarks and, of course, fishing marks. In most cases they will put you right on the fishing 'hot spot' described. And the

The Western Entrance is the main thoroughfare for all species into and out of the Port.

The Stony Point pier is a very popular land based fishing location. During the summer months, it is very popular with anglers.

answer to your next question… Yes, they are my favourite fishing locations and hot spots where my customers, friends, local charter boat operators and I have found great fishing in the past. I have added a number of GPS marks from other people in this update. I did this because no one can claim to know it all and I wanted to give you, the reader, the most informative read possible. Special thanks to all my friends and colleges who donated their favourite fishing spots for you to enjoy. The secret world of fishing is finally starting to change and I am excited. At this point I must thank Colin Guilmartin, past proprietor of the Kilcunda Caravan Park for his extensive knowledge on the Eastern Entrance and the Rhyll to Elizabeth Island area. Not only is his knowledge vast, but he was more than happy to share it with you all. Fishing would be a better fraternity if all of its members had Colin's attitude and passion for the sport. And to all of the anglers that I have come to know over the past two decades, thank you for teaching me and allowing me the honour of sharing some of your best fishing spots through the donation of your favourite GPS marks for this publication. Through your help this edition of Fishing Western Port really has become the 'bible' on this area that you just wouldn't leave home without.

Remember to always use common sense, as marks given are sometimes only a guide to the area. It will be up to the individual to use a depth sounder to find the perfect location once arriving in the general vicinity of the GPS mark provided.

FISHING REGULATIONS

To ensure that future generations have the opportunity to enjoy all that Western Port has to offer, Fisheries Victoria, a division of the *Department of Environment and Primary Industries*, aims to sustainability manage our fisheries resources for the entire community.

To help Fisheries Victoria ensure 'Fish Forever' recreational anglers are required to comply with a range of catch limits, including minimum legal lengths, bag and possession limits, and closed seasons.

Fisheries officers who regularly patrol Western Port encourage anglers to pay particular attention to the size and catch limits for gummy shark and school shark, which are measured in a different way to most scale fish.

These regulations are put in place to protect the fishery and to ensure it thrives for future generations to enjoy. Before any fishing outing, make sure you have a valid Recreational fishing licence and keep a copy of the latest Victorian Recreational Fishing Guide for information on size limits, bag limits, closed seasons, marine parks etc. in your boat or tackle box. It can be viewed online by visiting *www.depi.vic.gov.au/fishing* or you can download the app through you're app store. Alternatively, you can pick up a hardcopy, free of charge, from DPI regional offices, selected tourism outlets, one of more than 900 recreational fishing outlets in Victoria or by calling the Customer Service centre on 136 186. It is also important to note that these rules are constantly changing, so make sure your information is up to date.

Fisheries Victoria welcomes reports of suspected illegal fishing activities anywhere in Victoria. Just telephone 13FISH (133 474) with helpful information such as time, date and location, a description of the people involved, vehicle and boat registration numbers, the type of activity and the equipment being used.

My advice is to take only what you need, don't bag your limit, instead limit your bag. The fun in fishing doesn't come from taking home buckets of fish. It is all about enjoying time and experiences on the water with family and friends. If you need the measuring stick to check if a fish is of legal size, it probably isn't worth taking, and if you always carry a digital camera, you can even let the big ones go and still hold the memories forever.

Big calamari are highly prized in the Port, Finding them can be a challenge. Expert anglers like Spotters sunglass representative Jason Portelli know the ins and outs of where they can be found.

CHAPTER 2
FISH SPECIES
OF WESTERN PORT

The Middle Spit is the most well known producer of whiting in season. Charter operators such as Aleks Matic from Reel Time Charters know just how productive the area can be.

KING GEORGE WHITING (SILLAGINODES PUNCTATA)

Western Port certainly is famous for its King George whiting fishery. These relatively small silver white and gold spotted fish, fight hard, taste great and are fairly easy to locate and catch if you follow a few simple rules.

They are available to anglers on the Port year round, but the traditional 'whiting season' runs from Mid December through to through to the first frost in May. School fish around 25–30 cm tend to dominate early in the season with bigger fish coming in greater numbers from March onwards. Whiting can grow up to an inch a month in the right conditions, so if you find a good patch in April, you may be in for some seriously good fishing.

Whiting are a school fish that obviously travel in numbers and prefer to work the edge of shallow or exposed mud and or sand banks. Anglers usually target them in the shallows in depths ranging from 3–6 metres, but this can vary depending on the location, stage of the tide, time of year etc. It is simply a matter of giving it a go for 10 to 15 minutes maximum and then moving on if you have no joy. There is no point moving 5 kilometres to find them. Try leapfrogging your way along the bank, stopping every 50–100 metres until you hit the jackpot. A proven technique is to simply let out more anchor rope and drift with the tide to a new sand patch, once happy with the spot, tie off the anchor rope and try again. This will allow you to cover an area without having to start and boats motor possible spooking the school.

Even though these shallow banks are the traditional home of whiting, they are found in every extremity of the Port and for that

reason the can literally turn up anywhere. Even land based anglers can get in on the action.

In recent years since the introduction and acceptance of braided super lines, a deep water whiting fishery has emerged producing greater numbers of bigger fish or channel whiting as they are known. Many anglers now target whiting in 10–25 metres of water with success. You will have to work the tides to your advantage, but the rewards are huge. I have seen bags of 20 whiting with fish ranging from 45–52 centimetres. They are serious whiting in anyone's book. The average size of whiting taken in the Port ranges between 27–35 cm with fish around that size attaining an average weight of 250–350 grams. However, some of these deep water fish and fish from areas like Balnarring and Cat Bay can push 50 cm plus and often approach the magic two pound mark (908 g in the new scale). One kilo whiting are often talked about, but I reckon the Port would be lucky to see two genuine one kilo fish a year on average. A one kilo whiting has to be over 50 cm in length and in excellent condition to make the weight. Many come close, but very few make the grade.

The Western Port Angling Club has held the Whiting Challenge for over 15 years in prime whiting time. On the weekend comp, in conjunction with Paul Worsteling's Tackleworld Cranbourne they offer a $1000 cash prize for the first whiting weighed over one kilo. It has only gone off once in almost 20 years, and that fish went 1005 grams.

The thing that I love about whiting is that they are not a difficult fish to catch when the correct techniques are used. They will often

KING GEORGE WHITING

school in big numbers and bite aggressively when competing for a feed.

As far as eating qualities are concerned, few fish rate close to King George whiting. The succulent white flesh melts in your mouth and has to be in the top three fish I have ever tasted. In my opinion, the only fish that even come close are flathead, Tasmanian trumpeter and blue-eye trevalla.

In relative terms, whiting are only a small fish and therefore only light gear is required. Most anglers use a 2 – 4 kilo line on a 1000–2500 size spin reel. I like to use something like a Shimano Nexave or Exage as they are silky smooth and will give angling pleasure season after season. Whiting fishing can be tough on reels, especially in the deeper water, so it is worthwhile spending a few extra dollars to get a good one. The best rods for this use are normally 6–9 feet (2–3 m), with an ultra-sensitive tip. Most anglers prefer to use a nibble tip rod with a light tip for bite detection and shock absorption and a stiff butt section for lifting power. The length of the rod is also important. Simple principles of biomechanics would indicate that a long rod picks up more line when striking a fish than a short rod does. When you consider that both actions take exactly the same amount of time to complete, it makes sense to go for the longer rod and hook more fish. I use a Shimano Prowler for deep and fast water and the new Prowler Light for shallow slow moving water.

When you look at the anatomy of a whiting (especially the mouth) you can see that it is a bottom feeder. Keeping this in mind, it is important to use a rig that stays pretty much anchored to the bottom. In saying this, it can be helpful to keep the bait moving by bouncing it up and down, a technique also known as tea bagging. Slowly retrieving the bait along the bottom is also a very effective technique used.

A paternoster rig is used by 95 per cent of all whiting anglers with the choice of a one or two hook rig dependent on personal preference. However, there are several variations to a standard paternoster that are also used successfully throughout the Port. My advice is to experiment until you find the one that works for you.

When making your rig it is important to use a fluorocarbon leader such as Nitlon. This line is dense, does not absorb water and is almost invisible in water. It is also much more abrasion resistant than normal mono, which makes it perfect for the working end of your rig when fishing over rough bottom or when the picker fish like toads and leatherjackets are around.

The whiting rig is usually fished in conjunction with a bomb (teardrop) or torpedo sinker with the weight kept to a minimum at all times. One to two ounces is standard. Hook size and style will depend on the individual with size 6 long shank patterns by far the most popular. In saying that, I have seen a huge trend moving towards circle style hooks, with Owner light Mutu hooks now on most whiting fishos shopping list. The beauty of the circle hook is that the fish will hook themselves and that they rarely swallow the hook. It nails them in the lip in 90 per cent of cases. If you are looking for a more traditional hook, then stay with a Mustad Bloodworm. Two small orange beads and 3 cm of pink tube threaded on the line and allowed to run freely so that they find their way down to sit just above the hook will certainly increase your catch rate. This adds colour to the natural bait and works extremely well in all conditions.

Few anglers choose not to tie their own rigs due to eyesight restraints or lack of their own knot tying ability. This is where pre-tied rigs take out all the hard work for an angler. Today, pre-tied

Western Port is famous for its quality King George whiting.

rigs are much more advanced than some 10 years ago. Quality control has increased tenfold and the components they are made from are that of the finest found from any major fishing tackle supplier. One such rig is the Instinct Whiting Prowler Rig. A two dropper paternoster which is tied from 15lb fluorocarbon leader. Fitted with two red beads on each dropper arm, a size #6 circle hook and some flashing for the attractant. Might I say, never in my history of owning a tackle store have I seen such a shift towards anglers purchasing pre-tied rigs and in the 2012/13 whiting season, our local weekly fishing report at *www.ifish.com.au* clearly showed this rigs popularity and effectiveness with which how many anglers reported their catches using them.

The most popular whiting baits are pipis, mussels, sandworms, pilchard, bass yabbies and squid. A cocktail combination of two or more of these baits can also be very effective at times.

It is crucial that you berley to firstly draw these fish in and then to hold them at the boat. I like to use a stainless steel mesh pot filled with pellets that I lower to the bottom. Pellets by themselves work well but for greater success, mix in some pilchards and pour a small bottle of tuna oil over the concoction. Once on the bottom, the fish and tuna oil will create an oily slick that will drift along the bottom with the force of the tide. I would not go whiting fishing without berley, as I would feel as though I was wasting my time.

SNAPPER (PAGRUS AURATUS)

For many decades the whiting fishery in Western Port has overshadowed its great snapper population. The truth of the matter

Nothing beats catching snapper in the Port. Author, Paul Worsteling displays a lovely fish caught from Rhyll late in the afternoon.

is that the snapper have always been there, but anglers just never knew when, where or how to catch them.

In the late 1980s and early 1990s anglers started making the move from Port Phillip Bay across the peninsula to Western Port in search of snapper. The lure of larger fish saw them working hard to locate new areas and learn new techniques. It may seem strange now, but it was a scary transition to make all those years ago and those anglers were pioneers that have opened the Port up to what is today.

It is no secret that the Port is the place to find big snapper. I have personally weighed over 40 snapper over 20 pound while working in my tackle store in Cranbourne during the past eighteen years. Of these fish, over 90 per cent have come from Western Port and less than 10 per cent from Port Phillip Bay. If you want the trophy fish, Western Port is the place to find it.

Western Port always leads the charge when the snapper arrive these days. Being a smaller waterway with more shallow areas than that of Port Phillip Bay, the overall temperature is always a little higher. The warmer temperatures aid in speeding up the snappers metabolism, hence more fish are caught early in the season. Snapper start to filter into the Port in early to mid August with solid runs of fish occurring from September onwards. October and November tend to be the most productive months as fish aggregate with spawning in mind. The snapper fishery continues with numbers of fish taken through to May and scatterings of fish through to early June. In short, you can catch snapper with some reliability from September to May.

The hardest thing about catching snapper, like so many species, is finding them. Use the marks provided in this book, as they are a great places to catch snapper, because they have worked in the past. Fishing is not an exact science. Just spend time on the water where you find the type of fish you are chasing and follow the guidelines in publications such as this.

You will need a serious rod and reel, normally of the overhead variety to handle the punishment of big tides, sinkers and fish. Shimano IFISH Western Port and Shakespeare Tackleworld Exceed Ugly Stiks are ideal for the job. They are around seven feet long with a soft to medium tip and plenty of power through the butt.

Buy a good quality overhead reel capable of holding at least 300 yards of 30 pound Fins braid and you are in business. Though overhead outfits have their place in Western Port, a shift towards spin combos has become increasingly popular in recent years. Reels have increased in quality and prices have dropped considerably for the technology included in the body of the reel. A spin outfit should be able to hold 300 yards of 30 or 50lb fins braid and support a good amount of drag pressure. Shimano's Exage 8000 or a Saragosa 10,000 model will fit the bill matched to a Shimano IFISH Western Port or one of the new Shimano Pelagic Nano Series. They really have taken fishing rod technology to the next level.

The rig is complex, so take note of the diagrams provided. A running sinker clip slides on the main line (braid) and is stopped by a black rolling swivel forming the start of the trace. (Avoid brass swivels as they are too big for their breaking strain and they do not swivel under load.) Completely remove the stainless steel clip on the slider and replace it with a 20 cm length of 6–8 kilo line with a loop on the bottom for your sinker. This will keep your bait just off the bottom and break away if your sinker becomes snagged. This way you won't loose your whole rig and, more importantly, your fish. Sinker size will vary from 2 to 20 ounces with bomb or teardrop shapes the way to go. They have no corners and therefore won't spin as much in the current.

Your trace should by 40–80 pounds, with 60 preferred, and at least 1.2–1.8 metres long, but no longer than the distance from the reel seat to the rod tip. If it is any longer it will make landing fish a nightmare—I learnt this the hard way. Try two chemically sharpened 4/0–8/0 hooks depending on the bait, with a snelled rig extremely effective in holding baits straight in raging tides. In saying this, a single hook is a handy tool in a small strip bait fished on a locked drag. Use either a Shinto 6041 Spear Point or Hiroi Light circle hooks depending on your situation. As with using circle hooks for whiting, for snapper, gummy shark and elephant fish they are no different. In fact, circle hooks work best in locations of tidal variance. Due to the tide pressure and in conjunction with a braided fishing line, the hook can set itself without angler interference, the perfect components to any equation.

The most popular baits for snapper in Western Port include pilchards, sauries, squid, scad, striped tuna, barracouta and whiting heads or fresh fish fillets from anything from Australian salmon to rock cod. If you can catch your own bait it is always a bonus, but freshly frozen baits still account for the majority of big snapper catches.

Always remember that the two most crucial factors related to catching snapper are PERSEVERANCE and PERSISTENCE. If you have these two qualities, then everything else will eventually come your way.

If your dream is to one day catch trophy snapper of 10 kilo plus then you are on the right track in trying to learn more about Western Port. There is nothing in the fishing world that compares to landing your first, or any, big snapper for that matter. Good luck and I hope that this has helped you on your way.

GUMMY SHARK (MUSTELUS ANTARCTICUS)

Western Port is the home of what I regard as the best big gummy shark fishery in the country and possibly the world for that matter. There might be more big fish somewhere out there in the big blue ocean, but I am unaware of it and if no one can fish it with regularity, then it doesn't really count anyway.

Anglers in the UK would go off their tree if they could experience the gummy fishery that we take for granted. Over there, gummies are called smooth hound and a six kilo fish would stop the nation. Then again, so would a banjo shark, a smelly eel and a big carp. We are so blessed in Australia.

There are two tricks to finding gummies. First, you can anchor your boat at the mouth of a channel that branches into several other blind channels just before the high tide. If you stay here through the run out to low tide, you will encounter gummies from this entire area that have slipped off the banks to avoid being left high and dry. This way you are fishing a huge area and not just the 100 square metres at the back of the boat. This system will funnel the fish to you. In that, berley is your best friend and along with the tide, will bring fish from far and wide due to the smell. Sure, you will also encounter some of the largest sting-rays ever seen but as I always say, "if you're not hooking them, you're bait isn't on the bottom". The downfall to hooking sting-rays is that you could bust your tackle if it is not up too the task and or rig as well as being tight to an unwanted species when a gummy swims into your berley trail. It is for these reasons, fishing tackle has to be up for the task. This is why fishing 50lb fins braid and an 80lb bite leader is a great idea. It will tire over the unwanted's quickly having you back in the water with a fresh bait in no time.

The second technique, which is super effective on big to monster gummies, is to find any drop-off along a main arterial or channel. Think of a drop-off as a gutter on an open road. When it rains, leaves, rubbish and debris flow into it and are forced with the water to a drain. Western Port channels are no different. When the current

flows, any crab, dead fish, discarded bait etc: is pushed off the banks and down into the bottom edge of the channel where it is funnelled along until it becomes wedged amongst weed or in rock crevices or eaten by nearby fishes. Simply anchor on the contour line and sit it out. If you use the right bait, the sharks will come to you.

In just one month in 2006 we weighed over 20 gummies in the 15–25 kilo bracket and the key factor that rang true in over 90 per cent of catches was cured eel fillet baits. Cured eel has changed the fishery for the better. It will make an average fisho a very, very good angler in seconds. From zero to hero with a simple piece of bait. It has a unique smell and the gummies will swim a country mile to find it. Just stay put, be patient and they will find you with their incredible sense of smell. Even though eel is amazing, squid, striped tuna, pilchards, sauries and fresh fish fillets still account for their fair share of gummies. Depending on where you are fishing some baits will actually perform far better than others so always have a few at your disposal. In recent years, keen kayak anglers have been pushing the boundaries in Western Port and many have found that when fishing over the shallow flats, Banana Prawns are without doubt the number one bait.

Use the same gear and rig as outlined for snapper and you will have a great battle on your hands. If I can ask one favour in return for the advice I offer, this would be to release the big gummies. All the big fish are female and are quite old. They enter the Port to reproduce and are therefore a crucial link in a positive fishing future for this species. Take a picture and let her go—I promise you will feel great.

ELEPHANTS (CALLORHINCHUS MILII)

I had my first elephant experience in April 1987 while fishing with a mate off Lang Lang (The one and only time I launched at Lang Lang boat ramp), I wouldn't advise this today.

We caught three elephants of around four kilos each that day and I was blown away. Several years later elephant numbers in the Port started to increase until we had an absolute invasion in the early nineties.

They are neither a fish nor a shark, hence the reason I just refer to them as elephants. They actually fall into a small category of fishes known as chimeras, mainly because they share fish and shark-like characteristics and perpetuate their motion through their large pectoral fins.

They have a tail like a rat, a spike like a rhino horn on their head, pectoral fins like giant butterfly wings and of course a trunk like an elephant.

Elephants enter the Port in early to Mid March and then disappear as quickly as they showed up in early to mid May. The season may only last 8–10 weeks but it sure is full on.

Even though they can be found throughout Western Port, the 'Elephant triangle' is the place to find them. This is located by drawing an imaginary triangle between Corinella, New Haven and Tortoise Head. Fish anywhere within it and you are almost guaranteed a good session on these fish.

The fish cause a real commotion during this short season with literally thousands of anglers targeting them like shift workers, working around the clock.

Although they will eat just about anything, pilchards and squid work best. They respond well to berley and grow to 8 kilos, with average males weighing in at a kilo and females at around 2.5–3.5 kilos. A bag limit of three fish per angler was imposed in 1999 to eliminate ridiculous catches of up to 100 fish by single anglers. By 2006 elephant numbers were declining for reasons unknown and the Department of Environment and Primary Industries (DEPI) made a change to the fishing regulations on elephants to just one (1) elephant per recreational fishing licence holder per day. In turn, fewer anglers specifically target elephants today as they once did and they tend to focus on other species such as whiting. If they catch an elephant as bi-catch, it is normally returned unharmed. Some will head out with ultra light tackle and spend the time catching and releasing elephants for sport. That is always a great way to spend a few hours on the water.

This is a great species for teaching the basics of angling to juniors as the action is thick and fast and the fish put up a serious effort on any tackle. Most fishos use snapper gear for these fish, but if you want to have some serious fun put a snapper trace and rig on your whiting rod and hang on. Almost any rig will do the job but elephants are built to sniff out baits such as molluscs which hide under the soft slit and mud, hence your baits need to be on the bottom. A running sinker rig is best offered and tie it from 40lb trace. Elephants have quite small mouths so small baits are necessary. Hooks should also be kept small, a Shinto Hiori light circle 3/0 will suit best as setting a hook using light tackle is difficult and can result in a bust off.

Remember, the horn or "spike" on the top of their head is erected when they feel threatened. If you intend to keep an elephant for the table, break 1cm off the spike with a pair of pliers to prevent being punctured by it. Though they are not poisonous, the spike does contain bacteria which can cause infection. If the wound is not treated immediately, you'll be in for a great deal of pain.

MULLOWAY (ARGYROSOMUS JAPONICUS)

This is yet another fishery that has developed to the stage where anglers can actually target mulloway on Western Port with a reasonable chance of success. In the past, mulloway were only ever caught as a by-catch when fishing for species such as snapper or gummies.

The last decade has seen good numbers of mulloway within the Port with average fish size ranging 3–13 kilos. Bigger fish have still been elusive but in saying that we have seen fish in the 20–30 kilo plus bracket common and larger fish caught on the odd occasion.

There is no doubt that the Corinella area is the place to find them and I theorise that this is so because this is where you will find big numbers of flounder, one of the mulloway's favourite foods.

These fish should be targeted around specific moon phases with the full moon cycle popular with those in the know. Make sure that while targeting mulloway, you are fishing when a tide change is due to occur, at least two hours either side of the change. Use a snapper outfit and rig, but don't be scared to upsize the leader and hook size to suit big baits. In saying that, it always pays to fish a variety of baits and have them of varying sizes; you'd be pleasantly surprised at how effective a calamari ring can be on these elusive beasts.

When it comes to jewfish, fresh bait is best. Squid is a favourite along with fresh fish fillets from a variety of species. Live salmon,

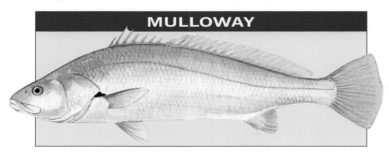

mullet and pike also work well. If you want to catch mulloway be prepared to fish long and hard and think about what you are doing at all times. Don't be scared to fish a big bait either. A 2 kilo live salmon is just a snack for a 30 kilo jewfish.

There are many locations to fish for mulloway and although Corinella is the most popular, specific locations such as Elizabeth Island, Snapper and Pelican Rocks, the Mosquito Channel and Spit Point are where more time and effort should be put i

FLATHEAD (VAR.)

Definitely one of the most underrated species in the Port is our humble old flathead. They are rarely targeted by anglers and normally caught on oversize baits intended for snapper, gummies and elephants.

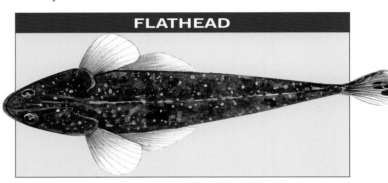

The beauty of the flathead is that they are accessible to everyone and can be found throughout Western Port. Their depth range varies from 5 cm of water on the sand flats of Somers to 50 metres plus off Kilcunda.

They are sensational eating, normally easy to find in numbers and have been caught at over 8 kilos in the Port. The average size flathead comes in at 25–35 cm with fish in the 40–60 cm bracket well worth searching for.

They will take almost any bait, as they are not that fussy. When you take a look at the flathead it is easy to see that they are true bottom dwellers and therefore baits should always be no more than 30 cm from the benthos.

Bigger fish can be targeted in shallower water with soft plastics whipped across the terrain. Just cast the lure out allowing it to sink to the bottom before whipping it up once or twice. Then let it sink back down, wind up the slack line that this created and repeat the process. If there is a flathead within range chances are you will catch it.

If targeting flathead with bait use a one or two hook paternoster rig with size 1–3/0 long shank or circle hooks. The rig itself doesn't have to be tied from too heavy leader but keep in mind the season in which your fishing, often there is quite a lot of by-catch such as pinkie snapper, elephants, gummy sharks and whiting. The wrong size leader could prevent landing one of these when bait fishing. Ideally, a 20lb leader should to the trick. They are notorious for swallowing hooks but the aforementioned will slow them down a bit. It is also better to drift over ground rather than anchor. Flathead are an ambush predator and wait for food to come to them. Those anglers fishing from the land tend to have high success on flathead from many locations around the Port. The flats at Silver Leaves become exposed at low tide and contain quite deep divots where flathead hide on the top of the high. Flicking soft plastics is very effective along here. The sandy coastline on Phillip Island from Cowes to Ventnor is also particularly productive.

When you catch one, handle it with care as they have some nasty spikes. A simple flattie flicker will save you a lot of pain in this area. I suggest you speak to your local tackle store about how to obtain one and more importantly, how to use it.

Big flathead travel in pairs, so if you ever see a big one caught or catch a big one yourself, its mate will usually not be too far away.

Australian Salmon (Arripis trutta)

AUSTRALIAN SALMON

Anglers choosing to target salmon are in for a good time all round. They can turn up at any time out of the blue, quickly turning an average day into a great one. Though they can be found year round in the Port, the prime months are April and May just before they head offshore and enter the surf zones for winter. Often the larger models are caught in the Western Entrance where the water is more turbulent and baitfish schools get rounded up and pulverised.

They are normally easy to spot with flocks of birds giving them away every time. When salmon feed, they push whitebait to the surface or into the shallows so that they can gorge themselves. This gives the birds a chance to get in for their chop and they rarely miss the opportunity of a free feed.

It is a great sight when the birds are working, the salmon are busting up and bait is leaping from the water in a last ditch attempt to escape with their lives. Just don't get too excited. Cruise over slowly and cut the engine when you are just within casting range. Don't drive into the school as you will put them down and they might not come back up. Soft plastics like Squidgy Flick Baits and Bass Minnows are deadly in this situation, as are metal lures.

Trolling also works well but is not as much fun as casting to the school. This is a good way of finding the fish if they disappear. One particular location to troll for salmon is in the region of Buoy 17 and around to Tortoise Head. Working depths ranging 5 to 8 meters along the edge of the bank is very effective with 100mm diving lures. Pike and Snook are also a popular catch here.

When Western Port's waters go cold over the winter months great salmon fishing can be had from Phillip Island and the Bass beaches.

The most common surf rig used by anglers in Victorian waters is the paternoster, which consists of two snoods to which hooks are attached with a third on the bottom of the rig for the sinker. A star sinker is used on a sandy bottom with a spoon sinker often used near reef or weed. Sinker weight will vary from 1 to 6 ounces, depending on weather conditions. Line size should range 6–10 kilos according to the angler's skill level and the size of sinker to be used. A long shank 1/0 hook is adequate for salmon taken along these beaches. It is also a good hook for other species and can be used with a wide variety of baits. Crabs can be a problem at times and like to steal baits placed on the bottom dropper of the rig. Replace this with a blue/white or red/white surf popper and wrap the top bait onto the hook with bait mate elastic to keep it from being taken.

When fishing from the rocks, a running float rig tends to work best with berley used to lure fish off the bottom towards the waiting bait. With the use of a float stopper, a leader of up to 5 metres can be used under the float without any confusion. A small sinker allowed to run freely down to the hook helps the bait to get through the water column, thus letting the float aid in bite detection.

Fish will range in size from 21 cm to over 4 kilos at times. If you intend to eat them, bleed them immediately and remove the dark flesh from the fillet before cooking.

Southern Calamari (Squid) (Sepioteuthis australis)

Big squid spawn in the Port from September onwards and it is no secret that the western shoreline between Flinders and the Tyabb bank is where you will find them in numbers. Calamari like a broken bottom consisting of weed, rock and small sand patches.

September is the prime time to target big calamari. It is not often you get to encounter a monster such as this.

If you are targeting them, try 1–3 metres to start with moving into deeper water if you have no success. You can cast a cloth covered prawn style jig, allowing it to sink so that it swims just above the structure on the bottom through the retrieve. These jigs can also be fished on a paternoster in deeper water or on a drop shot rig for deadly results.

One of the best ways to find big squid is with a whole silver whiting fished on a stainless steel squid jag. Fish this offering about 75 per cent of water depth below the float. The movement of the water's surface will give the whiting some action, bringing hungry squid from everywhere. When using baited jigs, berleying is an effective technique as calamari are attracted to the scent. Simply mash a few handfuls of pilchards into as fixed pot on the boats transom and let the baited jig float in the trail. It wont take long for a calamari to come along.

When you wind your bait in to check it, always look at the back of the head. Squid use their parrot-like beak to take nasty chunks out of their prey and it is often the only indication you will get that squid are in the area.

Another popular fishing technique is to enhance both baits and jigs with scented sprays. There are many different ones on the market but I prefer Stimulate. More recently has been the introduction of Ultra-Violet enhancers such as Spike-It. Calamari hunt using Ultra-Violet light and baits or jigs sprayed with this are devoured quite quickly when calamari are around.

Sharks within the Port

Not many anglers actually target sharks other than gummies within the Port, but plenty of sharks target anglers. At least one in five trips, and more probably one in two, your rig will be bitten clean off by a toothy critter. This will normally be a school shark, seven gill shark or a whaler shark. At the same time it could be a mako, thresher, hammerhead or white shark. They all call the Port home at different times of the season and will turn up where you least expect them.

If you intend to target sharks you will need some serious gear

There are many species of shark that can be caught in Western Port and Bass Strait. Mako sharks are the most highly prized.

in the range of a 10–24 kilo outfit. Match the trace to the outfit and the size of the bait you intend to use.

It is always a tough decision to know what size wire to use for sharks as it will put some species off, especially schoolies and hammerheads. The best thing to do is to always use the lightest wire possible, but understand that you may be bitten off by Mr Big.

The same running sinker set up can be used as for snapper and gummy shark with a wire trace attached to a snap swivel at the end of the line. For the bigger sharks a minimum of 3 metres of 170 pound wire should be used with a couple of 8/0–11/0 Owner Big Game Jobu hooks. The majority of these sharks feed on the bottom, so a large sinker will be needed.

Best baits for sharks within the Port include cured freshwater eel, tuna flesh, fresh fish and their fillets, sauries and squid.

When embarking on a shark session in the Port, you don't always have to look down the Western Entrance where some might think. At certain times of the year, the Top End channels such as the Tooradin, Bouchiers and Boultins channels produce some extremely big Whaler sharks. School sharks are often encountered in the Corinella, Elizabeth Island and Western Entrance and the odd Mako has been caught off Rhyll. All these specific locations are worth sitting out a tide and waiting.

Sharks Offshore

Fishing outside for sharks can be thrilling, with anticipation being a large part of the experience. Fishing for big pelagic sharks such as makos, threshers and blues can best be described as long periods of boredom interspersed with brief periods of mayhem.

Because there is less current to deal with offshore, a berley trail can be used to lure pelagic sharks (those sharks that feed predominantly in the upper layers of the water column) towards your waiting baits. This allows the use of lighter line for more sporting anglers.

The main targets offshore will be threshers, makos and blues with the occasional bronzie, hammerhead and white pointer popping up out of the blue…so to speak!

Most people don't berley anywhere near enough. If you want results, go hard or go home. In relation to berley, more is less when you are talking about laying a good trail over a six to eight hour period. During this length of time with an 8kt wind, you could travel around 13km's. Even though pilchards will take most of these species, they can be hard to keep on the hook when couta and squid are on the job. Striped tuna, eel, couta, whole squid, mackerel, sauries and salmon are all excellent baits and will all work on their day. You will also require a few baits on hand, particularly throughout January, February and March when arrow squid are in the peak numbers. Baits don't often last too long when they are around and they destroy them leaving nothing in minutes. Regular baits checks will be required.

Baits should be presented at varying depths from just off the bottom to just under the surface and from just behind the boat to about 100 metres down the trail. Hopefully having a good spread will find any fish that comes in for a look.

Traces will vary from 170 pound wire for threshers through to 400 pound for big makos and you will once again need tackle in the 10–24 kilo range with 15 kilo adequate for 99 per cent of cases in Bass Strait.

It is important to remember that this is a dangerous pastime as you are dealing with large wild animals that won't be at all happy with proceedings. Do not go offshore with an inexperienced crew. Take an expert the first time or go on a charter. There is often no room for error and you don't want to risk serious injury in search of a fish.

Always be careful when heading offshore as Bass Strait can be a big nasty place in a small trailer boat when the weather gets ugly. Try to fish in teams of two boats with up to four anglers per boat. If you hook a big fish you will need all hands on deck.

It is interesting to note that 11 a.m. has been nicknamed "shark o'clock" for pelagics. I have lost count of how many bites I and others have had fifteen minutes either side of this prime shark time. Be ready around 11 a.m. and have good baits in the water, as chances are that the action isn't far away.

Knowing where to go is the most daunting task as it is a large expanse of water in Bass Strait. It has always been the assumption

to head out wide to 70 meters of water but this is not the case. In all cases, pick your wind direction and speed and try to set yourself up so the wind pushes you back to the direction from which you came. This will not work all the time but in most directions other than a north, north east, or north westerly they will. When choosing a location to begin, try to setup the drift to cross the bottom contour lines where upwelling might occur. Contour lines can have currents push baitfish along them in which predatory fish such as sharks might be in tune with. Switching their focus to a smelly berley trial is what will cause them to find you're offerings.

OTHER FISH ENCOUNTERED IN WESTERN PORT

The reason I was first drawn to Western Port was because of the variety of fish that it offers. When you put a bait down you never really know what you might pull up next. It is that lucky dip aspect that I have come to love and also that you can change your plans in a heartbeat and be off targeting another species within minutes. The following species are all available if you want to chase them.

Barracouta will find you and they will cause plenty of grief with their sharp teeth. They have strong oily flesh and silver skin, making them an excellent bait for most big fish. Snapper and gummies love whole couta heads. A metal lure fished on a short wire leader is the best way to catch them. They range from 15 cm to over a metre and at that size they are great fun to catch. Trolling small diving lures is also effective when dragged along the edges of shallow reef systems.

Leatherjackets are usually taken by anglers fishing for whiting and other species. The first indication you usually have of their presence is a small bite followed by a missing hook. Their teeth are tough and sharp and they have the power to bite a hook in half. When this happens I go to a much larger long shank hook (up to a size 1 or 1/0) and try to set it on the first bite. They are hard to target but offer excellent eating qualities. They are usually found near weed or rocky outcrops.

Flounder are found in many areas in the Port in huge numbers with Corinella and Coronet Bay the hotspots. Even though they are netted by professionals in large numbers, they are rarely taken by anglers on rod and reel. The best way to target them is with a prawn light and a spear when there is little or no moon in the sky.

Snook and pike are two totally separate species that are often confused by anglers. Snook tend to be much longer and rounder in the body than pike. A snook has a body shape more like a garfish while a pike is more like a barracouta. Pike rarely grow over 50 cm, whereas snook grow to well over a metre. They are both taken by trolling deep diving lures and baits such as gars on gang hooks. Metal lures towed behind paravanes also work well. These fish are rarely targeted, but offer great sport and a lot of fun. They are found throughout the Port in excellent numbers.

Mullet are a big hit for land based anglers who fish the many piers and inlets that the Port offers. Mullet feed best on the flood tide as it makes its way up inlets such as Deep Creek, Sawtells and Rutherford. Fishing along the Middle Spit is a popular area for mullet also. A small piece of pilchard or whitebait fillet fished on a size 8 long shank hook will work well under a float or on the bottom. These fish respond well to berley.

Garfish are also plentiful in the Port but with the fast tidal flow, they may be hard to target at times. You will often encounter them when you are fishing for whiting near weed beds. Of the most popular locations to fish for Gars, try Sunken Island between Lysaghts and the Middle Spit, Dickies Bay at San Remo and the Stony Point pier.

Simply anchor your boat on the bank edge and use a float set up with a size 10 long shank hook. Small silverfish and peeled prawn are ideal baits, although bread dough mixtures are also used with success. A fine berley including tuna oil will be needed to attract these little acrobats. Keep rigs light using only 3lb leader where possible. Varying sized hooks will work but for maximum hook penetration, the fine gauge Shinto Long Shank #12 is ideal.

Rock cod are taken all year round in both the deep and shallow waters and are a clear indication that the water is too cod for fish like snapper. They are basically bad news. I am not a fan of these slimy fish, but those who understand more about cooking fish than I do tell me that 24 hours in the fridge firms up the flesh and they are excellent to eat. Sorry, but I'm going to have a steak instead if that's okay.

Other species that are taken, but are of little edible value include the stingrays, shovel nose, Port Jackson shark, draughtboard shark, banjo shark, poisonous toad and porcupine fish.

Yellow-eye mullet might not be a highly prized species to catch but they are in abundance throughout the Port and offer excellent angling opportunities.

CHAPTER 3
BAITING & RIGS

It is not always easy understanding Western Port's waterway. Fishing on a local Charter is a lot of fun and can aid in teaching you a lot.

TAKE A CHARTER FIRST

Now that you are fully aware of the bounty that this amazing Port has to offer, one of the best pieces of advice that I could give you to learn more about fishing on Western Port would be to take a fishing charter with a qualified skipper and fishing professional. What you can pick up in a day on a charter with the right crew could take you twenty years to learn on your own. Book a trip and ask as many questions and observe all that you can. This will be a positive investment in your fishing future. Even today, I still like to go on charters on the Port to keep me up to speed with what the experts are up to. After all, they fish the Port every second day, so they should have a fair handle on things.

The following list of charter boats comes to you highly recommended by me. I am not being paid for this or getting any special favours. I just believe after twenty years of personal experience that these are people that I can trust to find you fish. Their skippers have also been kind enough to donate some of their favourite GPS marks to this text.

In alphabetical order-

Ace Fishing Charters	**Reel Adventure Fishing Charters**
Capt – Steve Johnston	Capt – Phil Wasnig
03 5979 1002	0409 932 077
0412 578 811	
	Reel Time Fishing Charters
Peninsula and Western Port	Capt – Matt Cini
Fishing Charters	0438 302 093
Capt – Robin Grey	
03 97695544	
0418 559 228	

TIME TO BAIT UP

I have seen anglers head out onto the Port with nothing but a block of pilchards when chasing snapper or just a bag of pipis when they have whiting in mind. The first question that comes to mind that I must ask, is what if the fish don't feel like the only bait you have on board that day?

Now I know that snapper love pilchards and whiting love pipis, but I love steak and I sure don't feel like eating it every night.

Just as financial advisers continually tell us, it is important not to put all your eggs in one basket. So if you take that advice on board, you wouldn't put four pilchard baits out and sit back waiting for Mr Snapper to come along.

Variety is the spice of life, so mix it up a bit. What about a pillie on one rod, followed by a saurie, a whole squid and a fresh salmon fillet on the others. As soon as you see a trend emerging, you can switch your bait options in that direction. Even if you land five snapper and they all take squid, my advice is to leave at least one alternative bait in the water. I have often done this with a much larger bait and found success on bigger fish in the school.

Your choice of bait will often determine how productive your outing will be, so it is well worth putting some good thought into it. I find it is best to take a good selection of fresh frozen baits from your local tackle store and then complement this by catching whatever you can during your outing. Squid, garfish, mackerel, salmon, flathead, couta, trevally, bass yabbies etc all make excellent baits and can be found throughout the Port

For a host of species

Bait presentation is also very important to avoid the tide from ruining your offering and your chances of catching a fish. Poorly rigged baits will spin in the current, twisting around their longitudinal axis, thus alerting fish to their non-natural status. Each bait should be tested in the water beside the boat and be modified if necessary before being lowered to the bottom. When a bait looks good in the water, it is enough to get you excited without even catching a fish.

CATCHING FRESH BAIT IN WESTERN PORT

PILCHARDS may be one of the most popular purchased and used baits but with it's varying tidal flow, Western Port supports a wide variety of smaller species which can be caught and used fresh for bait. Species such as King-George whiting, yellow tail scad, silver trevally, yellow-eye mullet, slimy mackerel, barracouta, pike, snook, garfish and calamari are all worth catching to use.

These species can be caught right throughout the Port but specific locations such as along the Middle Spit, around the Submarine at Hastings, Tankerton Jetty and along the edge of the bank which runs between Stony Point ramp channel and Hanns Inlet are the most productive.

Catching bait is relatively easy and basically comes down to using berley and the right tackle. It always pays to have a light rod on board and some berley. Take the time to give it ago before a serious snapper or gummy shark mission.

The ideal rig for most of the above mentioned species is a paternoster with size 10 long shank hooks. Use the lightest sinker weight as possible. As for berley, a stainless steel pot with adequate weight to hold it directly on the bottom. Fill it with mashed pilchards and you'll soon attract a variety of species right to the back of your boat. Small pieces of pipi or pilchard fillet make top baits for any of the mentioned species.

THE BEST BAITS

If pilchards were actors, they'd win every golden Globe award available. Being so readily available and dynamite for the more highly prized species, they are cost effective, easy to get your hands on and most importantly, they work. A pillie will produce snapper and gummies of all sizes, flathead, salmon, squid and even big whiting. There is not a fish that I can think of in the Port that won't eat a pilchard, so you should always have them on board.

When buying pillies look for IQF fish. These are individually quick frozen and tend to be better than fish in blocks and only about 20 per cent more expensive.

SQUID is one of the best early season snapper baits whether it is fresh or frozen. Every species loves it and, because of its tough nature, it keeps the pickers at bay a bit longer than soft baits like pilchards. Big gummies, mulloway and whiting have a particular preference to squid.

SAURIES are a beakless oceanic garfish that have huge oil content. They work well on all large predators as the oil creates a self-berleying slick. They can be used whole, halved and filleted.

GARFISH can be caught on location in the shallower parts of the Port and like a little weed for protection. They make excellent snapper baits both frozen and fresh and can be baited in similar ways to sauries.

CURED EEL has been one of the biggest finds in fishing in recent times. Even though people have used it for years, the masses only

The elusive mulloway is sought by many but few catch them. Mark Keaveny caught this prized model after many hours.

There are many different baits to use in Western Port but fresh calamari is undoubtedly the number one for a wide range of species including snapper, gummy sharks and whiting.

got onto it when I started to promote it through my weekly fishing report at www.ifish.com.au midway through the 2005–2006 season. It is without doubt the greatest gummy shark bait you can use. A small fillet will draw a gummy from kilometres away and stay on your hook like an old piece of boot leather. Snapper are about the only other fish that eat it and you can catch several fish on the same piece. It is almost too good to be true.

PIPIS AND PILCHARDS are two of the most commonly used baits for a variety of fish on the Port. However, remember that variety is the spice of life and always have a good selection of baits on offer.

STRIPED TUNA is the bait that lured the biggest snapper I have ever caught on the Port. Gummies also love it as do several other species. I don't believe enough anglers give it a go and miss great opportunities because of it. It has a strong oil content and lets the fish know it's there. It can be soft, thus making it hard to bait up at times, but it is well worth the effort. Sharks of all varieties just love it.

SILVER WHITING are one of the best snapper baits in Port Phillip Bay but rarely get a mention in Western Port. They are a tough bait and well worth a look prior to Christmas. Few anglers know this but silver whiting can be caught in both entrances into Western Port and in Bass Strait. As fresh baits, they are outstanding.

FISH FILLETS, heads and frames account for big numbers of fish like snapper, gummies and seven gill sharks. Salmon, couta and trevally are all very popular but be sure not to discount flathead, cowanyoung and even rock cod. The key to fishing a fillet is the way you rig it, with a fixed second hook the secret. The top hook secures the bait and holds it in place with the bottom hook just pinned under the skin ready for the strike.

PIPIS are a must for any visit to the Port as there isn't a fish alive that wouldn't eat one. Whiting anglers use them as their number one weapon in search of these tasty fish. They are readily available, freeze well, open easily and the shells make excellent berley. When using them for whiting it sometimes helps to put a small strip of squid on the hook first. The whiting will steal the soft pipi easily and when it comes back for the squid, he's yours.

MUSSELS are also an excellent whiting bait but they have faded in popularity a little because of the work involved in getting them out of the shell. The trick is to shell them the night before, so that when the whiting are on, you can make the most of the hot bite by keeping baits in the water. I think a mussel will out-fish a pipi most of the time. I often use mussels until I get the fish going and then switch to pipis. A cocktail of both baits on the same hook also does the job.

BASS YABBIES are another excellent bait that is well worth the effort to collect or buy. If you use a bait pump over the shallows at low tide you will normally find more than enough for a day's outing. Locations such as the Middle Spit, Rutherford Inlet and any other soft mud bank will produce Bass Yabbies. Just look for their holes and put the pump down the same area two or three times. Fish like whiting simply love them.

When targeting such species as gummy sharks and snapper, fresh and oily fish heads and or fillets are very hard to resist.

BELOW: When the snapper are on, it can be standing room only, especially around the corals.

BERLEY BASICS

Berley can best be described as any foreign substance introduced to the water to attract and stimulate fish to feed. It can be as elaborate as a pre-packaged delight with hormones added to drive the fish crazy or as simple as some left over, old, stale bread. Regardless of which end of the spectrum it falls, one thing is for certain—it works. All species will respond to berley, but they all have to be approached in the right way. Whiting like pellets presented on the bottom that slowly break up or mashed pilchards placed into a pot and left to sit on the bottom. This will not only draw fish to your area, but also hold them there. Makos, on the other hand, respond well to minced fish flesh and pilchard cubes soaked in tuna oil. A long steady stream will eventually bring one in for a closer look.

No matter what species you are chasing, the basics of berley remain constant. A little often rather than a lot all at once, and make sure you keep your berley within strike range. Don't throw a heap of pilchard cubes over the side in the middle of the tide and expect them to do anything positive.

Berley pots will help with both of the above points. Secret Weapons and a similar blue plastic pot allow you to send berley to the bottom before opening to release it directly on to the grounds you are fishing. Onion bags and fixed lid mesh pots are also handy, as they can be filled with berley before being lowered with the anchor. I like to use light cord or heavy mono as the attachment because they are often eaten by sharks, and when this happens you want them to let go quickly. This system works well because the berley runs directly under your boat and past waiting baits. This way you get the benefit from your hard work, instead of berleying for the boat anchored 100 metres away.

When the tide slows I also like to throw about a kilo of cut baits and cubes that have been soaking in tuna oil for over half an hour over the side. They will sink straight to the bottom and sit there dispensing oil until the tide picks up and slowly rolls them past your baits, creating a great trail for fish of all species to follow back to the source.

Berley is so good that I refuse to fish without it. Spend some time researching berley and berleying techniques for your next trip and I guarantee you will improve your catch.

DOWNRIGGING

A downrigger is a device used to get baits down through the water column. This works well when trolling or when the tidal influence is severe. A large lead weight (up to 8 kilos) is lowered to the desired depth on heavy wire. A release clip is attached to the back of the downrigger bomb and your line is held in place by the tension of the clip. When a fish strikes, the clip releases your line and the fish can be fought on a flatline unhindered by a sinker. This system has several distinct advantages. It makes it possible to fish through an entire tide, leader lengths are limited only by your imagination and it is far more enjoyable fighting big fish without the drag of big sinkers. The use of downriggers has increased steadily over the last five years and in time to come they will be just another standard accessory for the keen Western Port angler. Anglers using downriggers often comment on the "humming" sound given off but the force of the current causing the wide to vibrate. Some say it is off putting to fish but don't you think a boat motor, or a thousand boat motors might spook a snapper school a bit more? Though it could be possible, there is a solution. Rather than using the wire, strip it off and either replace it with 200 lb braid or 130–200 lb specifically manufactured downrigger braid. Being finer in diameter compared to that of the wire, the "humming" will be limited.

WESTERN PORT RIGS

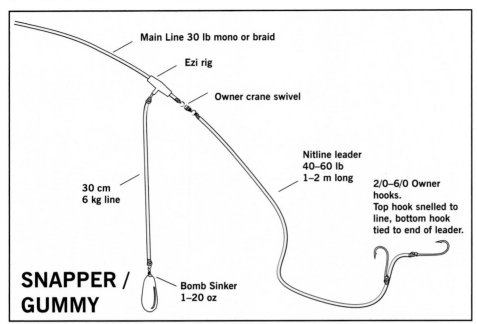

Main Line 30 lb mono or braid

Ezi rig

Owner crane swivel

30 cm
6 kg line

Nitline leader
40–60 lb
1–2 m long

2/0–6/0 Owner hooks.
Top hook snelled to line, bottom hook tied to end of leader.

Bomb Sinker
1–20 oz

SNAPPER / GUMMY

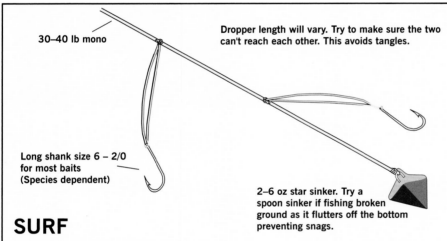

30–40 lb mono

Dropper length will vary. Try to make sure the two can't reach each other. This avoids tangles.

Long shank size 6 – 2/0 for most baits (Species dependent)

2–6 oz star sinker. Try a spoon sinker if fishing broken ground as it flutters off the bottom preventing snags.

SURF

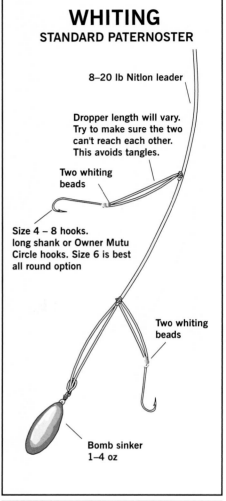

WHITING
STANDARD PATERNOSTER

8–20 lb Nitlon leader

Dropper length will vary. Try to make sure the two can't reach each other. This avoids tangles.

Two whiting beads

Size 4 – 8 hooks. long shank or Owner Mutu Circle hooks. Size 6 is best all round option

Two whiting beads

Bomb sinker
1–4 oz

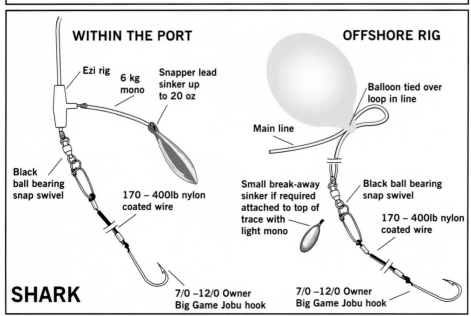

WITHIN THE PORT

Ezi rig   6 kg mono

Snapper lead sinker up to 20 oz

Black ball bearing snap swivel

170 – 400lb nylon coated wire

OFFSHORE RIG

Balloon tied over loop in line

Main line

Small break-away sinker if required attached to top of trace with light mono

Black ball bearing snap swivel

170 – 400lb nylon coated wire

7/0 –12/0 Owner Big Game Jobu hook

7/0 –12/0 Owner Big Game Jobu hook

SHARK

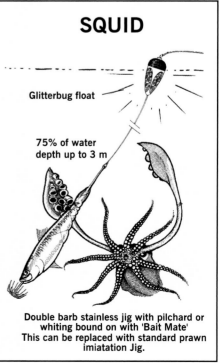

SQUID

Glitterbug float

75% of water depth up to 3 m

Double barb stainless jig with pilchard or whiting bound on with 'Bait Mate' This can be replaced with standard prawn imiatation Jig.

CHAPTER 4
BOATING IN WESTERN PORT

When boating in channels and around the edges of the Port always keep a good lookout for channel markers and moored vessels.

BOATING PRECAUTIONS

Most anglers are scared of Western Port—or perhaps terrified is a better word. They have visions of mud banks and sandbars just jumping out in front of them and being stuck for days. Even though there is an element of risk, and even danger, these factors can be controlled somewhat through knowledge and experience. As I always say—there are only two types of people that fish on Western Port, those who have run aground and those who will.

You can do a few things to keep the odds in your favour. I cannot recommend strongly enough the purchase of a GPS mapping system for your boat. It will save you hours of pain, big dollars on fuel and help you to investigate parts of the Port that you never knew existed. The message is simple, get one and you will become a better angler. If the budget doesn't allow, then good charts and a book like this one are a great start.

If you are exploring or on the Port for the first time, try to take someone out who is experienced or take a charter to learn a particular area. The other tip is to explore on the flood tide rather than the ebb, If you do get stuck, you want the water to be coming in and not going out as this could be the difference between a 10 minute or ten hour wait stuck on the mud.

It is also important that you understand the navigational markers or 'street signs' of the water as they are designed to keep you out of harms way. Make a point of memorising them and you will navigate the Port with much greater confidence, Port Pile Marker (RED)

Keep the Port Side mark to your left when going upstream and to the right when going downstream. Remember that on the way in, 'there is never any red port LEFT'. Starboard Pile Marker (GREEN) Keep the Starboard Side mark to your right when going upstream and to the left when heading downstream.

ISOLATED DANGER

Submerged reef and rocks are clearly marked around the Port by a cardinal mark displaying two large black balls on top of a pile. This signals isolated danger. Avoid these areas at all times as it is likely that on the high tide the reef is only just under the water. On low tide the reef is normally visible. You can clearly see an isolated danger marker located on Eagle Rock.

CARDINAL MARK

A cardinal mark indicates deeper water in the direction shown, either north, south, east or west. Cardinal marks can be used in conjunction with a compass to find a safe passage. These marks should be learnt and remembered.

Wind Against Tide

Wind against the tide is one situation that visiting anglers have to get a grasp of quickly. Put quite simply, if the wind is blowing in an opposite direction to which a strong tide is flowing, the waves will literally stand up on end causing treacherous boating conditions. When planning your day take the tidal flow and wind direction into account before heading off for long distances. What may have been a ten minute cruise in the morning could easily turn into a two hour battle in the afternoon. This is not intended to scare you, but just to make you think and plan to save any preventable mishaps.

Areas that are badly effected by this situation are Settlement Point to Snapper Rock at Corinella, between Red Point and the Middle Sand at the Eastern Entrance, at the Narrows under the San Remo Bridge and in the Main Channel. Take special care in these areas. Always keep in mind the weather conditions and how much fuel you have on board your boat. Changing conditions like wind against tide may see you use a lot more fuel than you bargained for. Running out of fuel is never a good situation.

Boating Rules and Regulation

A Victorian Recreational Boat Operator Licence is required to operate a registered recreational powerboat in all Victorian waters. Contact your local Vic Roads Customer Service Centre or call 13 11 71 to book a test. More information is also available at www.marinesafety.vic.gov.au or call them on 1800 223 022. Copies of the Victorian Recreational Boating Safety Handbook are available free and can be obtained from retail boat yards, tackle stores and Vic Roads offices.

Never leave the ramp without the full complement of safety gear outlined in the handbook and always remember that a mobile phone could be your best asset in an emergency. Just call 000 and give the operator your co-ordinates off the GPS. This will pinpoint your location for rescuers.

New PFD (lifejacket) rules were also recently introduced in Victoria and must be fully understood before your next outing or a hefty fine may come your way.

Beating the Tides

Fortunately, technology is on the side of the angler when waging the battle with Western Port's raging tides. Braided lines, downriggers, chemically sharpened hooks, vastly improved rod and reel technology and Internet, teletext and fish finders that give tidal information years in advance, all work in the favour of the keen angler. Knowledge is power and that power is now available on tap. And if a bad tradesman always blames his tools, then you simply have no excuse in the 21st Century not to have a thorough understanding of tidal movement.

Western Port fills and empties through two passages, one at the Nobbies (Western Entrance and larger opening), the other at San Remo (Eastern Entrance and smaller opening).

Due to the fact that there are two openings between the Port and Bass Strait and that one of them is quite big, an extremely large volume of water enters and leaves during each flood (run in to high tide) and ebb (run out to low tide). This is why the tidal flow is so fast when compared to Port Phillip Bay, which has only one relatively small opening.

Due to the fast water movement, tides from different directions meeting, wind against tide, which causes short, sharp, dangerous seas and eddies that cause water to swirl, Western Port can be an eerie place. Again, knowledge is power and when you understand why this is happening and how to avoid or deal with each scenario you can get on with the serious business of catching fish.

As mentioned earlier, the Western Port tides are a science that must be fully understood before fishing success will be mastered. Unfortunately, many of us are forced to fish only when time allows and this is not necessarily when the time is right. The timing of your trip on Western Port is essential if you expect results. Not only do some species feed better one hour either side of the tide change, but due to minimal tidal influence, this is when you can use the lightest possible sinker to get the bait into and keep it in the strike zone.

Experience has shown that the low tide and the start of the flood often produce more fish, but this is dependent on the area and the species you are targeting. One benefit of fishing the low tide that can't be overlooked is the fact that there is less water for the fish to hide in. As the many shallow areas drain, fish enter the channels where you can be ready and waiting in ambush.

Even though most fish still prefer some run in the water that the tide creates, too much tide will be detrimental to your fishing, thus these instances are best avoided. The trick is to fish a high, low tide coming up to a low, high tide. This will ensure minimal water flow and therefore, increased fishing time. This also gives you the opportunity to fish into the tide phase for a longer period. When

The main reason boaters are apprehensive to fish the Port is due to the shallow banks which become exposed at low tide. Fear of running aground keeps a lot of anglers from venturing out.

Due to the land mass surrounding the Port, boats of all sizes can get out in most weather conditions.

the run is not as fast, you may be able to fish in the same spot from one tide, right through to the next. The best bite time may well be at mid tide, which you just couldn't fish on the bigger tides of the week or month.

In simple terms—if the difference between the morning high and low is half a metre and between the afternoon high and low is one metre, and both tides share the same time frame (about six hours between high and low) then it is obvious that the tide must move twice as fast in the afternoon scenario between the peaks. Therefore, it would be best to fish the morning tide on this day. Not only will the tide move slower, allowing smaller weights and the ability to fish almost anywhere, but it will also allow you to fish for much longer periods of time and possibly even through the entire tide. Note: The Herald Sun newspaper provides a daily guide to high / low tides times for Stony Point along with many websites such as www.ifish.com.au, which not only gives up-to-date fishing reports for Western Port, but also has links for tidal information.

Free tide charts are also available from all good tackle retailers.

- Tidal Differences from Port Phillip Heads
- Flinders Jetty subtract 5 minutes
- Kilcunda add 10 minutes
- Newhaven Jetty add 30 minutes
- Cowes Jetty add 51 minutes
- Corinella add 58 minutes
- Stony Point add 60 minutes
- Hastings Pier add 67 minutes
- Warneet Jetty add 84 minutes
- Tooradin Jetty add 106 minutes
- Lang Lang add 115 minutes

The direction and strength of winds may alter these times and it must always be remembered that tidal information is a prediction, not a fact. If winds should hold a tide up due to strength, remember the following tide will hasten to regain that time. This is important when crossing a bank on an ebb tide and must be taken into account

when putting boats on trailers at certain ramps. Poor planning could leave you high and dry. It is also important to note on this point that there are only two types of anglers on Western Port, those who have run ground and those who WILL! Don't let the fear of embarrassment keep you from enjoying one of the country's most fascinating waterways.

Not all channel markers are easily visible and not all contain lights at night. When boating on the Port always take your time and be careful.

CHAPTER 5
WESTERN PORT BY MAP

MARINE NATIONAL PARKS

Western Port has three national parks, which are off limits to all fishing activity. They are The Churchill Island Marine National Park located between Rhyll and New Haven on Phillip Island, the French Island Marine National Park located along the northern shoreline of French Island and the Yaringa Marine National Park situated on Watson Inlet to the west of Quail Island. The boundaries are marked with yellow buoys in the water, by land at the high water mark and with GPS co-ordinates.

All forms of fishing including line, spear, net fishing, commercial and catch and release are prohibited in these zones. Shellfish collection, bait collection and marine aquaculture are also banned. Basically, if you intend to fish, stay away from the Marine Parks. For more information on these areas go to *www.parkweb.vic.gov.au* or contact the Parks Victoria Information Centre on 13 19 63.

WESTERN ENTRANCE

This area has grown in popularity over the past decade as anglers push further south in search of quality fish. With the excellent gummy sharks and solid runs of snapper often available along the width and breath of the main shipping channel, it is not hard to understand why this large body of water is attracting so much attention. Due to its oceanic nature, good fishing is often encountered with a large variety of species on offer.

WHERE TO FISH

This area is renowned for producing excellent numbers of monster calamari with September through to early November the most productive period.

Big spawning calamari move into the calm bays from Flinders through to Pt Leo to lay their egg cases over the shallow reefs. Squid to over four kilos can be encountered during these months with a fresh silver whiting suspended under a float on a barbed jig usually the most productive. These squid herald the start of the run of seasonal species such as snapper that also enter the Port at this time of year. When the big squid start to turn up of Flinders, you know the reds are not far away.

The majority of the bottom is lined with thick ribbon weed. Drifting over the top is deal, especially in 10 meters of water. If you can pick the right tide you'll be able to drift a good kilometre with ease and cover plenty of potential ground. Being open to the Bass Strait the larger calamari move into and out of the area and due to their size will respond well to larger size jigs. Ideally, size 3.5 and 3.0 artificial jigs will catch most of the squid. The current can push through this area quite fast at times. so rigging your jigs on a paternoster rig with a light sinker on the bottom is also a very effective technique.

Most of the whiting fishing in this area is carried out within a fairly close proximity to the Flinders Pier and the mussel farm. With clean oceanic water flooding in from Bass Strait the water here is usually very clean, making it quite easy to find good whiting ground. The area around the mussel farm is usually a safe bet from November through to mid January.

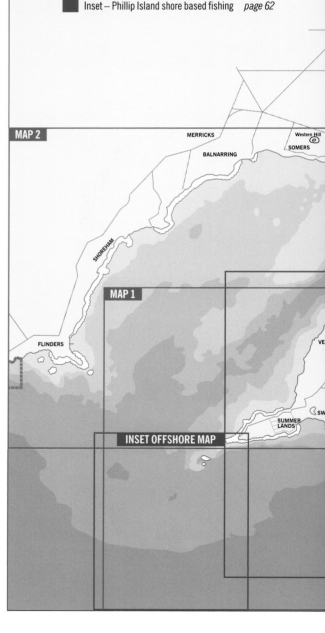

Quick Reference
Map Location Guide

WESTERN PORT MAPS

1 Western Entrance   *pages 27 & 28*
       Inset – Offshore Fishing   *page 27*
2 Balnarring (Outer West)   *pages 32 & 33*
3 East & North Arms   *page 36*
4 North Arm   *page 41*
5 Upper Western Port   *pages 44 & 45*
6 Corinella & Surrounds   *pages 50 & 51*
7 Eastern Entrance & Offshore   *pages 56 & 57*
       Inset – Phillip Island shore based fishing   *page 62*

MAP 2   MERRICKS   Western Hill   SOMERS
BALNARRING
SHOREHAM
MAP 1
FLINDERS   VE
SUMMER LANDS   SW
INSET OFFSHORE MAP

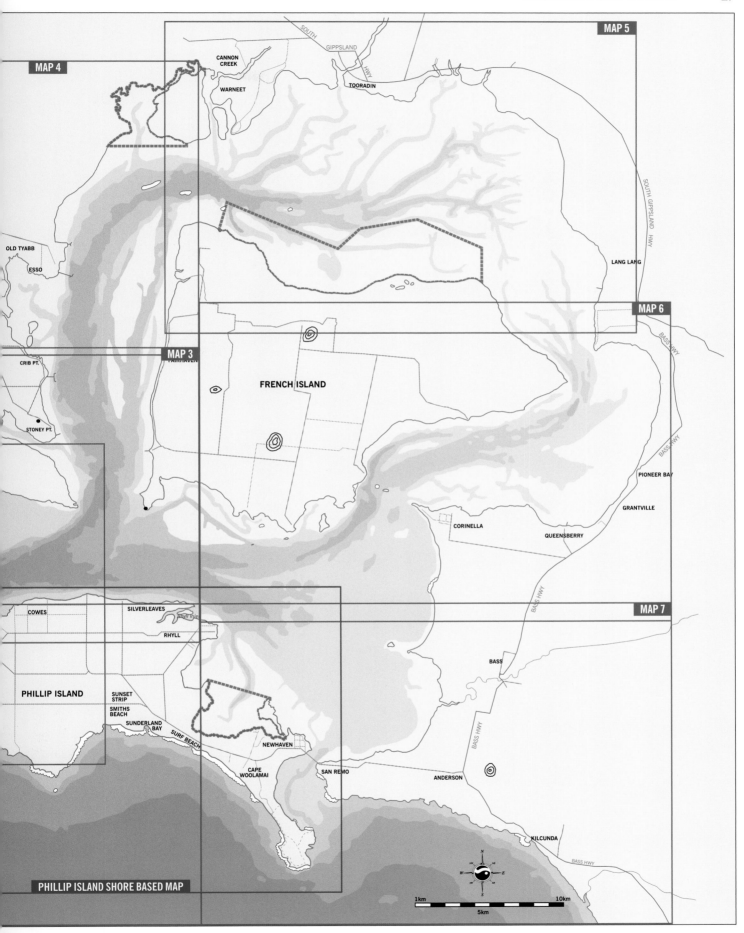

MAP 5

MAP 4

SOUTH
GIPPSLAND

CANNON
CREEK

WARNEET

TOORADIN

SOUTH GIPPSLAND HWY

LANG LANG

OLD TYABB

ESSO

MAP 6

MAP 3

FAIRHAVEN

CRIB PT.

FRENCH ISLAND

BASS HWY

STONEY PT.

BASS HWY

PIONEER BAY

GRANTVILLE

CORINELLA

QUEENSBERRY

COWES

SILVERLEAVES

Rhyll Inlet

RHYLL

MAP 7

PHILLIP ISLAND

SUNSET
STRIP

SMITHS
BEACH

SUNDERLAND BAY

SURF BEACH

NEWHAVEN

CAPE
WOOLAMAI

SAN REMO

BASS

ANDERSON

BASS HWY

KILCUNDA

BASS HWY

PHILLIP ISLAND SHORE BASED MAP

N
W   E
S

1km   10km
5km

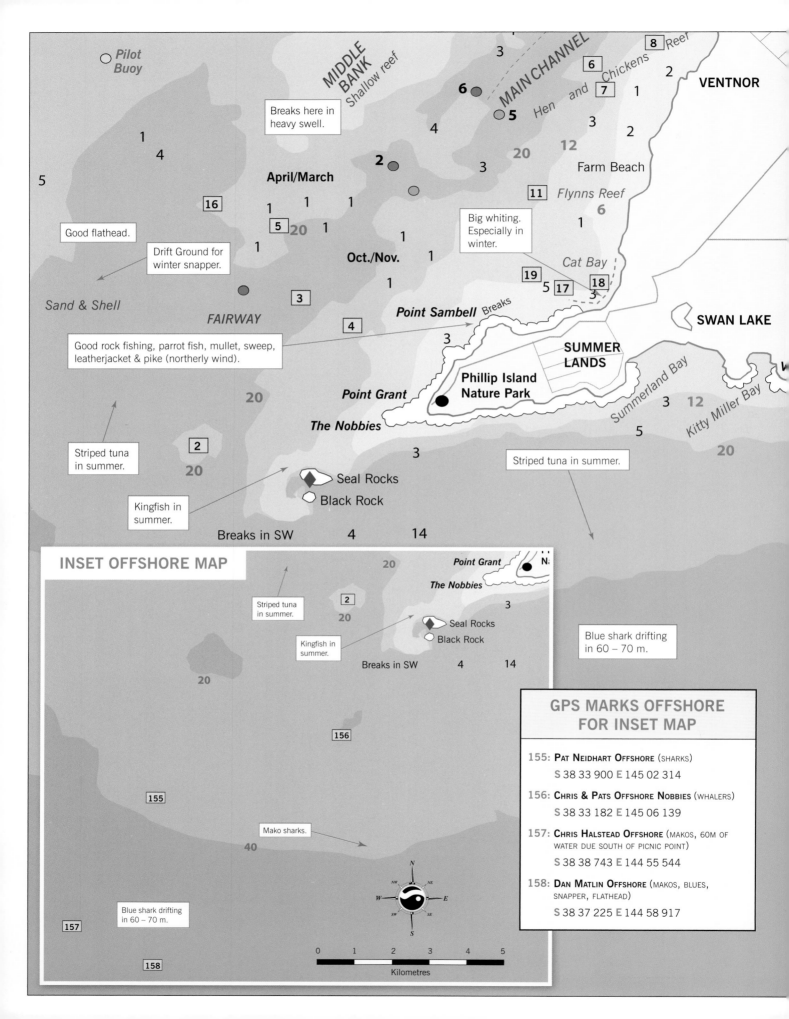

Pilot Buoy

MIDDLE BANK
Shallow reef

Breaks here in heavy swell.

1

4

5

16

Good flathead.

Drift Ground for winter snapper.

Sand & Shell

FAIRWAY

April/March

5 20

1 1 1

1

Oct./Nov.

1

1

3

3

Good rock fishing, parrot fish, mullet, sweep, leatherjacket & pike (northerly wind).

4

Point Sambell Breaks

3

Point Grant

Phillip Island Nature Park

The Nobbies

Striped tuna in summer.

2

20

20

Kingfish in summer.

Seal Rocks

Black Rock

Breaks in SW 4 14

3

3

MAIN CHANNEL

8 Reef

6

7

Hen and Chickens

5

4

6

2

3

3

20 12

11 Flynns Reef

6

1

Big whiting. Especially in winter.

Cat Bay

5 17 18

3

19

VENTNOR

2

1

2

3

Farm Beach

SWAN LAKE

SUMMER LANDS

Summerland Bay

3 12

5

Kitty Miller Bay

20

Striped tuna in summer.

INSET OFFSHORE MAP

20

Point Grant N

The Nobbies

Striped tuna in summer.

2

20

Kingfish in summer.

Seal Rocks

Black Rock

Breaks in SW 4 14

3

20

156

155

Mako sharks.

40

Blue shark drifting in 60 – 70 m.

157

Blue shark drifting in 60 – 70 m.

158

N
NW NE
W E
SW SE
S

0 1 2 3 4 5
Kilometres

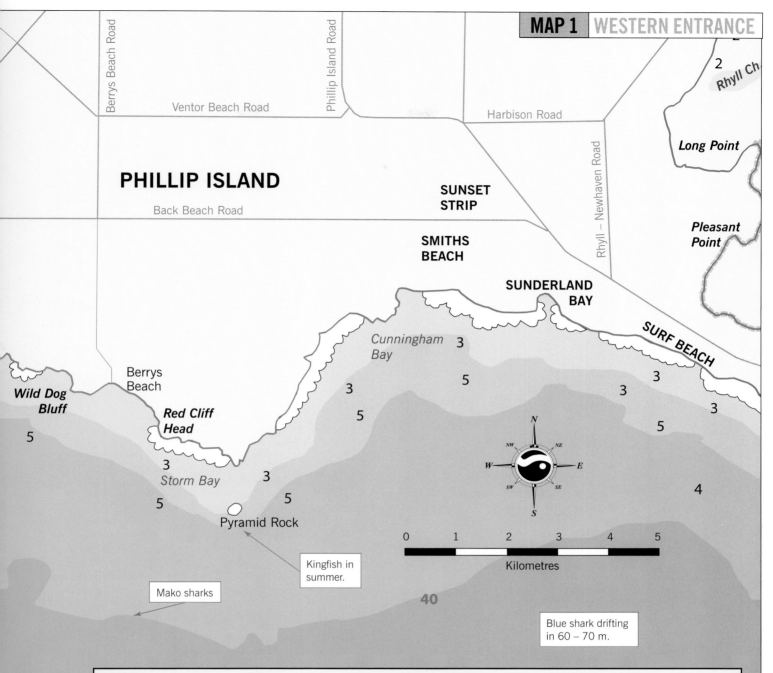

MAP 1 WESTERN ENTRANCE

2

Rhyll Ch

Long Point

Pleasant Point

PHILLIP ISLAND

Back Beach Road

Ventor Beach Road

Berrys Beach Road

Phillip Island Road

Harbison Road

Rhyll – Newhaven Road

SUNSET STRIP

SMITHS BEACH

SUNDERLAND BAY

SURF BEACH

Cunningham Bay

Berrys Beach

Wild Dog Bluff

Red Cliff Head

Storm Bay

Pyramid Rock

Kingfish in summer.

Mako sharks

Blue shark drifting in 60 – 70 m.

40

3 5 3 3 3 3 5 5 5 5 3 3 5 4

N NW NE W E SW SE S

0 1 2 3 4 5

Kilometres

GPS MARKS

2: WESTERN ENTRANCE: (EARLY/LATE SEASON SNAPPER, GUMMIES)
S 38 30 827 E 145 04 585

3: PATRIC NEIDHART: FAIRWAY BUOY: (GOOD SNAPPER, FLATHEAD)
S 38 29 973 E 145 06 056

4: PATRIC NEIDHART BUOY 1 (SNAPPER ,PIKE, REEF FISH, SHARKS)
S 38 30 206 E 145 06 818

5: PATRIC NEIDHART BUOY 2 (GUMMY, SMALL SNAPPER, SEVEN GILL)
S 38 29 317 E 145 05 971

6: ACE FISHING CHARTERS BUOY 5 (SNAPPER, APPROX. 23 M)
S 38 28 529 E 145 08 318

7: REEL TIME FISHING CHARTERS BUOY 5
(SEVEN GILL SHARK, SNAPPER, GUMMIES, SALMON)
S 38 28 594 E 145 08 309

8: PATRIC NEIDHART BUOY 5 (GUMMIES)
S 38 28 606 E 145 08 853

11: REEL TIME CHARTERS CAT BAY
(GUMMIES, PINKIES, SNAPPER, GOOD YEAR ROUND, BEST ON EBB TIDE)
S 38 29 062 E 145 08 125

16: WEST ENTRANCE (20M SNAPPER)
S 38 29 400 E 145 04 996

17: CAT BAY (WHITING)
S 38 30 168 E 145 08 419

18: CAT BAY (WHITING)
S 38 30 255 E 145 08 619

19: CAT BAY (WHITING)
S 38 30 269 E 145 08 473

While difficult to access due to lack of launching facilities, the Balnarring area can produce some magnificent fish and big calamari.

For the smaller boats, there is plenty of good fishing between the pier and Shoreham on the mainland shores. King George whiting, grass whiting, flathead and Australian salmon are taken as close as 100 metres off the shore between these points. I suggest you work along the shoreline, moving 50–100 metres at a time until you find fish. Berley will also help to find them and then to hold them at the boat.

The deeper water off Flinders is an untouched gummy shark and seven gill hotspot. It receives very little angling pressure, yet it produces excellent results. Very few people fish it and those that do keep it very quiet. Some even choosing to fish at night, hoping to slip in under the cover of darkness. If you spend the time learning to fish in this area you will be very well rewarded. Spend some time studying good charts and focus your efforts on the contour lines. Always be wary that this area is exposed to strong southerly, south easterly and easterly winds at times. In conjunction with that, a strong tide so always make safety the number one priority and not the fish. Research and experience pay dividends in this location.

Shoreham

Often when anglers refer to big whiting from Flinders and 'around the corner', they are in fact talking about Shoreham. As with Flinders, I believe it is relatively untapped when compared with other locations on the Port. This area has constantly produced the best bags of King George whiting that I have ever seen from the Port. If you are ever going to go in search of your one kilo Western Port whiting, then this is the place to start. Don't be scared to fish deep water and be prepared to move a lot. I have had days when ten moves have produced just one fish with the eleventh (for no particular reason) leading us to a solid bag of 42–49 cm whiting.

This area also produces consistent numbers of grass whiting 'stranger', snook, pike, flathead, pinkie snapper and big calamari. Most anglers access this area by launching from the beach at Flinders as it is a long run from Stony Point and you have to cross the Middle Bank. Fortunately, this has been made much easier with the aid of GPS mapping. Even with this technology, you still have to be careful as the channel is shallow, narrow and has a good dogleg. Launching at Flinders warrants the use of a 4wd as the ramp is sand and ocean swells can make it difficult. Many inexperienced anglers have had their car and boat swamped here, so be careful.

Snapper are caught in this region but they are not that common. Often, those anchoring and fishing for gummy sharks catch the odd red by surprise. Fish to 5 kilos have been recorded in the area but they are rare. Most of the area averages 5-10 meters and is a very productive location for gummy sharks. Concentrate on the bottom contour's and when a location is found, sit out an entire tide for best results.

The fishing can be exceptional along the edges of the Main Channel, with snapper, big gummy shark, school shark, whiting and flathead being the most popular species to target.

Fish the channel edges and depth contours for the best results but remember it is an offence to anchor in a shipping channel with non-compliance carrying a heavy penalty. Most of the good fishing is along the edge of the bank between the channel marker buoys and the Middle Bank itself. Work the tides and moon phases to your advantage with your freshest baits being deployed to the bottom an hour either side of a tide change.

Middle Bank

This bank starts out from Shoreham and follows the East Arm Channel north towards Sandy Point. It is considered one of the most dangerous stretches of water in Western Port. The water breaks all along this bank with a heavy swell and it is impossible to cross at low tide. It is also subject to short, sharp, breaking waves caused by wind pushing against the tide. The breaking water is visible from a long distance away and anglers are advised to keep well clear of this area unless conditions are ideal. If you are thinking of crossing the Middle Bank, always do it with someone experienced. Make sure you have a GPS onboard to mark you're path and always cross on a high tide when the wind is 5 knots or less and there is no swell. Just after buoy 12 there is an area in which you can access. As mentioned above, be very careful at all times.

Boat Ramps

The Flinders ramp is situated wherever you can find good hard sand between the pier and the tracks situated about 35 metres to the south. Launching can be carried out by reversing onto the solid sand. Local anglers prefer to launch with a tractor, but visiting anglers can launch and retrieve their boats from the sand with very few dramas. A high tide is the most suitable. A four-wheel drive vehicle is preferred. Be careful as swells can roll around the point and swamp your vehicle.

Land Based Fishing

The Flinders Pier (Melway Ref 262 B9) is located on The Esplanade and is a great land based structure that reigns supreme as the squid capital of Western Port. Its proximity to the ocean sees calamari to over four kilos taken between September and January and it is known as one of the best fish producing piers on the Port. The pier is stained black with ink and it is standing room only when news gets out that the big squid are on the chew. It provides good fishing for most of the year with September to January best. Night fishing from the Flinders Pier is most productive, especially during a flood tide. Calamari are targeted using a baited jig suspended under a float. Artificial jigs also work very well, particularly in a 3.0 size.

King George whiting, wrasse, stranger (grass whiting), leatherjackets and yellow eye mullet can all be taken from this popular land based haunt.

BALNARRING

This area is the centre of the East Arm Channel and within 5 kilometres of the ramps from Cowes, Stony Point and Flinders. Anglers from these ramps fish these waters regularly with good results. However, if you choose to fish from Balnarring, you will need to make contact with the local yacht club as this club controls the only ramp available. As this yacht club is not permanently operated, anglers from the Mornington Peninsula and Melbourne eastern suburbs may find it more beneficial to launch from Flinders or Stony Point having to cross the Middle Bank.

WHERE TO FISH

BALNARRING

Out from Balnarring, a channel runs in a winding southwest direction for 1 kilometre before emptying into the deeper water. This channel is marked with piles and produces some good fishing. Big King George whiting can be taken at any stage of the tide, as well as good sized flathead, grass whiting and wrasse.

If you only have a small boat and don't want to travel too far, you can fish this channel all day for your feed of whiting and also have the chance of picking up some small snapper on the change of tide. A drift in this area will normally produce better numbers of flathead.

This is also a very popular area for snook, with these fish taken in large numbers from October through to May. No marks are needed for these fish; simply troll the area with deep diving lures like Tilsan Barras and Hydro Magnums.

There are quite a few isolated reefs in the area, which hold good calamari throughout most of the year. A GPS mapping system will show these and it can be a simply as motoring up to the reef putting in a few casts and catch your quarry.

Kayak anglers can easily launch from the beach and access these points in a very short amount of travel time. Catching whiting from a kayak is also a lot of fun as they are quite easy to find here with the help of a little berley.

SOMERS

Somers is only a short distance from Balnarring and is fished with the same result although pike and snook are a little more popular in this area. This is where many of the biggest Western Port whiting reside. Just search for the sand holes among the weed with your polaroids and move constantly until you find fish.

MIDDLE BANK

If you intend to fish the Main Channel from Balnarring or Somers, care will be needed crossing the Middle Bank. Although possibly not as dangerous as further down towards the entrance, it can still be nasty. The channel that runs through the Middle Bank from Somers to the Main Channel is clearly marked on GPS mapping systems and should not be navigated without one unless you have a thorough understanding of the area. If you intend to fish the main channel I suggest launching from Stony Point or Hastings, as I always prefer to do a few extra kilometres in the car, rather than on the water. It may be fine heading out on the perfect morning, but you never really know what the wind will be doing when you are battling your way home.

MAIN CHANNEL

The Main Channel carries a large variety of fish, with all shark species and snapper being the most sought after. These fish can be taken most of the year with the prime time being from September until May.

The entire area from Buoy 17 through to the Fairway Buoy tends to be productive for different anglers at different times. Most anglers who find great success on the Port have one or two 'hot spots' in this area.

Early and late season snapper congregate on a small patch of broken ground about 750 metres southwest of the Fairway Shipping Buoy. Bag limit catches of big fish are attainable on a small hump that rises to 19 metres of water. Large gummies, seven gills and crayfish also turn up in this area on a very regular basis.

A great snapper fishery has also been discovered by the charter boat brigade in recent years. When officials tightened up on laws prohibiting anchoring in the shipping channels, skippers such as Steve Johnson and Robin Grey began to drift with their clients with excellent results. When the snapper are on, you will see dozens of boats drifting up and down the channel with plenty of bent rods. When they are on, it is not unusual for the charter boys to land between 50 and 100 snapper of 2–5 kilos.

There are literally hundreds of great snapper locations in this area and it is well worth doing some research to find a few of your own.

The last two seasons have also seen this area shine as the gummy shark capital of the world. This may seem like an overstatement, but I think it may be true. Gummy sharks of 10–30 kilos have become common rather than a rarity. The use of cured eel baits and better fishing techniques has seen this fishery explode. Charter operators like Matt Cini have made a career out of chasing big gummies and this is one area you will often find him soaking a few baits. To find potential locations, follow the bottom contour lines as if they are highways, this is where the fish will be travelling. Set anchor correctly and wait it out for a big battle. Due to the tide strength heavy sinkers are required to keep your baits on the bottom. The average sinker weight required will be 12 ounces, but when the tide is running, expect to use 20 ounces or more. If your bait isn't on the bottom, you'll have a stingray fest instead of a gummy one.

Good quality whiting and flathead are also taken on the edges of the channel from early November onwards and it is not uncommon to hook whiting up to 600 grams in this area with fish to 950 grams a pleasant surprise.

The shoreline from Cat Bay through to Ventnor will produce big whiting year round and has proven itself as an excellent winter fishery with whiting to 50 cm a real possibility. Big calamari, rock flathead and silver trevally also call this area home.

At various times throughout the year huge salmon schools move up this channel and are easily noticeable as birds follow and feed on

Jarrod Day displays a solid gummy shark caught while fishing out from Point Leo, a well known gummy haunt.

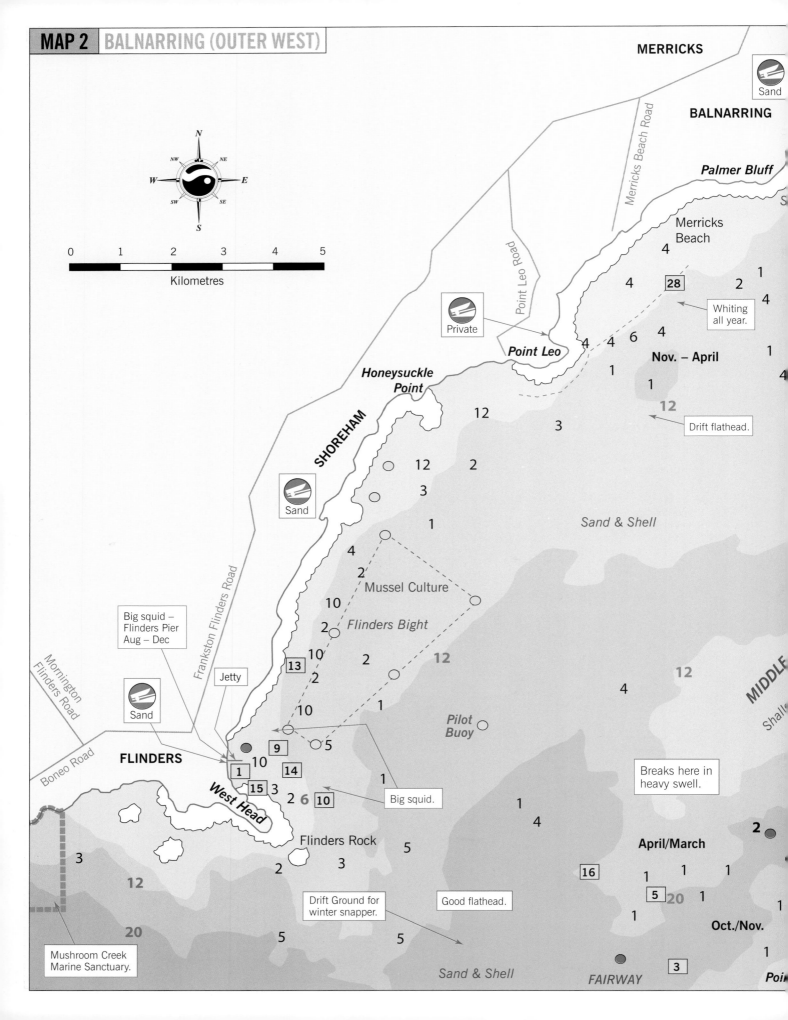

MAP 2 BALNARRING (OUTER WEST)

MERRICKS

BALNARRING

Palmer Bluff

Merricks
Beach

Whiting
all year.

Nov. – April

Drift flathead.

Point Leo

Private

*Honeysuckle
Point*

SHOREHAM

Sand & Shell

Sand

Mussel Culture

Flinders Bight

Big squid –
Flinders Pier
Aug – Dec

Jetty

Frankston Flinders Road

Pilot
Buoy

Breaks here in
heavy swell.

Sand

Mornington
Flinders Road

Big squid.

MIDDLE

Shalle

FLINDERS

Boneo Road

West Head

Flinders Rock

April/March

Good flathead.

Oct./Nov.

Drift Ground for
winter snapper.

Mushroom Creek
Marine Sanctuary.

Sand & Shell

FAIRWAY

Poi

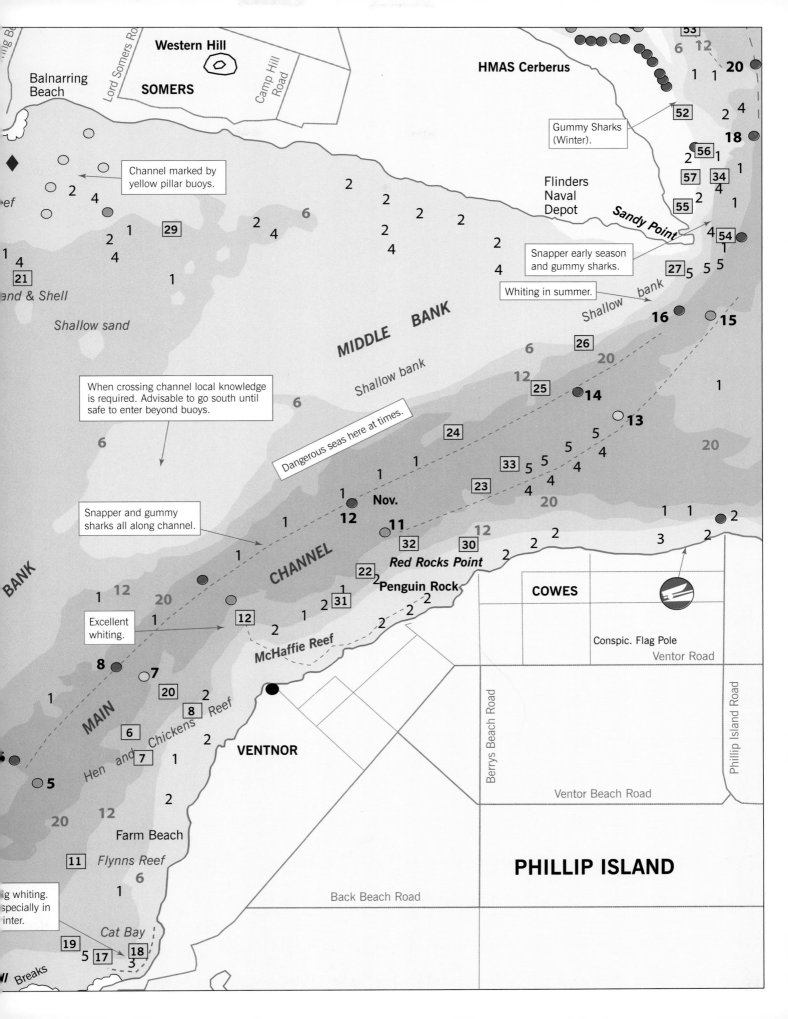

Western Hill

SOMERS

Balnarring Beach

Camp Hill Road

Lord Somers Road

HMAS Cerberus

Gummy Sharks (Winter).

Flinders Naval Depot

Sandy Point

Channel marked by yellow pillar buoys.

29

21

and & Shell

Shallow sand

MIDDLE BANK

Shallow bank

Snapper early season and gummy sharks.

Whiting in summer.

Shallow bank

16

15

26

20

When crossing channel local knowledge is required. Advisable to go south until safe to enter beyond buoys.

6

Dangerous seas here at times.

12

25

14

13

24

20

Snapper and gummy sharks all along channel.

12

12 Nov.

11

32

33

23

30

12

Red Rocks Point

22

CHANNEL

31

Penguin Rock

COWES

Excellent whiting.

12

McHaffie Reef

Conspic. Flag Pole

Ventor Road

BANK

MAIN

8

7

20

8

Hen and Chickens Reef

6

7

VENTNOR

5

Farm Beach

12

20

11

Flynns Reef

6

Berrys Beach Road

Phillip Island Road

Ventor Beach Road

PHILLIP ISLAND

Back Beach Road

ig whiting.
specially in
inter.

Cat Bay

19

17

18

Breaks

5

3

GPS MARKS FOR MAP 2 BALNARRING (OUTER WEST)

1: **Flinders Pier:**
S 38 28 570 E 145 01 709

3: **Patric Neidhart: Fairway buoy:** (Good snapper, flathead)
S 38 29 973 E 145 06 056

5: **Patric Neidhart Buoy 2** (Gummy, small snapper, seven gill)
S 38 29 317 E 145 05 971

6: **Ace Fishing Charters Buoy 5** (Snapper, approx. 23 m)
S 38 28 529 E 145 08 318

7: **Reel Time Fishing Charters Buoy 5**
(Seven gill shark, snapper, gummies, salmon)
S 38 28 594 E 145 08 309

8: **Patric Neidhart Buoy 5** (Gummies)
S 38 28 606 E 145 08 853

9: **Reel Time Charters, Flinders**
(Squid, good early Sept to early Dec.) Drift between:
S 38 28 494 E 145 02 118

10: **Reel Time Charters, Flinders**
(Squid, good early Sept to early Dec.) Drift between
S 38 28 601 E 145 02 157

11: **Reel Time Charters Cat Bay**
(Gummies, pinkies, snapper, good year round, best on ebb tide)
S 38 29 062 E 145 08 125

12: **Reel Time Charters Buoy 7** (Snapper, gummies)
S 38 27 267 E 145 10 158

13: **Flinders** (Whiting)
S 38 27 768 E 145 02 347

16: **West Entrance** (20m Snapper)
S 38 29 400 E 145 04 996

17: **Cat Bay** (Whiting)
S 38 30 168 E 145 08 419

18: **Cat Bay** (Whiting)
S 38 30 255 E 145 08 619

19: **Cat Bay** (Whiting)
S 38 30 269 E 145 08 473

20: **Hi 5** (Snapper, gummies)
S 38 27 554 E 145 09 590

21: **Reel Time Charters Balnarring**
(Gummies year round, full moon, plus whiting, wrasse)
S 38 24 852 E 145 08 204

22: **Patric Neidhart Ventnor** (Squid and whiting)
S 38 27 432 E 145 11 018

23: **Ace Fishing Charters Buoy 11** (Snapper, approx. 21 m)
S 38 26 660 E 145 11 694

24: **Patric Neidhart Buoy 12** (Gummies with squid on slack water)
S 38 26 321 E 145 11 589

25: **Reel Time Charters Buoy 14** (Gummies year round)
S 38 25 613 E 145 13 056

26: **Patric Neidhart Buoy 14** (Gummies ebb tide)
S 38 25 477 E 145 13 286

27: **Jarrod Day Buoy 16** (Snapper Aug–Oct, approx. 20 m)
S 38 25 063 E 145 13 793

28: **Michael Ketelaar Merricks sand patch** (Whiting, pike, gummies, snapper, squid)
S 38 25 008 E 145 06 224

29: **Michael Ketelaar Somers sand hole** (Whiting and flathead)
S 38 24 510 E 145 08 999

30: **Tankers** (Whiting)
S 38 26 811 E 145 12 817

31: **East 7** (Whiting and pinkies)
S 38 27 068 E 145 11 722

32: **Low 11** (Gummies and snapper)
S 38 26 587 E 145 11 945

33: **Patric Neidhardt Bouy 11** (Snapper)
S 38 27 086 E 145 10 803

34: **Reel Time Charters buoy 18** (Pinkies, snapper, small gummies)
S 38 23 936 E 145 14 500

52: **Ace Fishing Charters Hanns Inlet** (Whiting, approx. 11 metres)
S 38 23 483 E 145 14 204

54: **Reel Time Charters Sandy Point** (Gummy year round, snapper Sept–Dec, whiting and pinkies Dec–April)
S 38 24 509 E 145 14 303

55: **Peninsula and Western Port Charters** (Sandy Point Whiting and pinkies, Nov–March, approx. 14.5 metres)
S 38 24 346 E 145 14 333

56: **Whiting**
S 38 23 495 E 145 14 090

57: **Whiting**
S 38 23 697 E 145 14 150

---

the bait the fish are chasing. A small metal lure or soft plastic stick bait tossed into the school or trolled, will normally get you some great baits and an honest feed if the fish are bled upon capture. Pike and snook are also partial to taking a trolled lure and there are some very big models of these around. On a calm day, troll around Hen and Chickens reef and up towards Cowes pier past McHaffies Reef.

Winds

As this area is all open water, it is affected by winds of any direction. Keep a good eye on the weather and carry a radio with you for any updated forecast that may be issued. Check the forecast before leaving home on www.bom.gov.au, and don't venture out if conditions won't allow. This area is severely affected by wind against tide, so be sure to plan your trip with this in mind. A mobile phone used in conjunction with a GPS is also a valuable safety tool that should never be overlooked.

Shore Based Fishing for the Balnarring (Outer West) Area

For the shore based angler, the Balnarring area is an ideal spot with both great beach and rock fishing available. Areas such as Pt Leo Surf Beach (Melway Ref 257 B7), Point Leo Rocks (Melway Ref 257 C7), Merricks Beach (Melway Ref 192 H12) and Somers Beach (Melway Ref 193 J12) produce a huge range of species from King George whiting, grass whiting, flathead and salmon through to pinkie snapper, big gummy sharks and large sharks such as seven gills, whalers and threshers.

In an easterly wind direction, fishing from the beach at Cat Bay can lead to quality catches of pinkie snapper, gummy sharks, seven gill sharks and bronze whalers.

Ventnor Beach is popular with land based anglers in the summer months for both whiting and calamari.

EAST ARM TO COWES & NORTH ARM TO STONY POINT

ue to the popularity of Western Port's elephant fish, this area is one of the most heavily fished on the Port. It has excellent access from several good ramps and offers a huge array of species.

The East Arm has plenty of deep water access for snapper and shark fishing, so looking for whiting is not as simple as the upper Western Port region around Warneet or Tooradin.

As you are fishing in deep and exposed waters in this area, more care should be taken for all on-board. Being open to winds from all directions, you will need to keep a good eye on the weather. If a wind change is forecast, stay close to home and be prepared to return as soon as you notice any change in weather patterns.

WHERE TO FISH

STONY POINT

Situated at the southern end of the North Arm, just 5 kilometres from Hastings, this area is ideal for the angler not wanting to travel a long distance on the water. It is only a short distance from the ramp to the channel and fishing can be carried out within minutes of launching. It is also very centrally located in relation to many popular areas on the Port.

The southern end of the Middle Spit is located about 1 kilometre due east of the ramp and is distinguished by a south cardinal mark. A cardinal mark indicates that deep water lies in the direction shown, e.g. north, south, east or west. This bank is a great place to start looking for whiting, garfish and squid. This is also the home of the big channel whiting in season. Anglers working in depths ranging 8 to 14 meters tend to catch some thumping fish along here.

Tankerton Pier, Eastern Channel, Tortoise Head and Sandy Point are additional areas handy to Stony Point that all offer a variety of fishing from whiting to snapper and just about every other species encountered in the Port.

SANDY POINT

Although not recognised as a fishing area by anglers, Sandy Point can produce fine fishing. If you launch at Stony Point and head in a southerly direction, Sandy Point is at the tip of the mainland. A large stretch of sandy beach marks this area, with good whiting fishing found in about 5 metres of water. The buoy marked with letters SP signifies Sandy Point. Anchoring between the buoy and the beach can lead to gummy sharks over 20 kilos caught. This location is also productive for winter snapper in May. Fishes best on the last two hours of the run out tide.

It is also a top spot for shark and snapper in the deeper water around Buoy 17. Again evening and dawn are the most productive times, especially when in conjunction with a tide change.

TORTOISE HEAD

This area is a very popular spot with anglers launching from Stony Point, Cowes and Rhyll.

The deeper water lying to the west of Tortoise Head between French Island and Buoy 17 is a great early season snapper mark in around 12 metres of water. Just try to find a drop-off or contour line, which the fish will swim along as they move up and down with the tide.

A small shallow bay exists between Tortoise Head and the Tankerton Pier to the north. Large schools of salmon often herd whitebait into the bay and are quite easy to target once the birds indicate their position. Motor towards the school, then cut the engine and either cast metal or soft plastic lures or small saltwater flies on a seven to eight weight outfit into it. Trolling can be effective

Western Port is one of the more accessible locations to fish in all weather conditions, that is if you understand the wind direction and safest launching facility.

at times but engine noise often puts the fish down and scares them away. Anchoring with berley will also be effective if you can find an area out of the tide.

Trolling hard body diving lures between the mouth of Gardeners Channel and Buoy 17 is very productive for pike, snook and silver trevally. Work in 5 meters of water along the edge of the reef for best results.

TORTOISE BANK

The Tortoise Bank is located due south of Tortoise Head and extends in an easterly direction, running parallel to French Island, stopping just before Bird Rock. This bank provides the angler with ample angling opportunity as it provides not only a good shallow platform, but also a good drop-off into the deeper water towards Cowes and Rhyll. Snapper, gummy and school shark, mulloway and elephant fish are usually found in this area. A drift along the edge of the bank can also result in a good feed of flathead.

The bank itself is a great area to find whiting, particularly on the western side. Just move until you find them and berley to keep them at the boat. Over the years and with the removal of commercial netting, the weed growth has come back significantly. This has seen an influx of calamari move into the area, which can be caught on baited jigs while fishing for whiting.

GARDNERS CHANNEL

This channel forms the northern side of the Tortoise Bank and produces some excellent whiting captures. The area at the entrance to the channel has fished extremely well in recent years prior to and just after Christmas. The area is relatively well sheltered from poor weather and fishes well for many species most of the season. This area is particularly popular with anglers targeting elephants. Just anchor anywhere in the channel and they are bound to swim past in bursts.

The water here is often quite clean, especially on the flood tides,

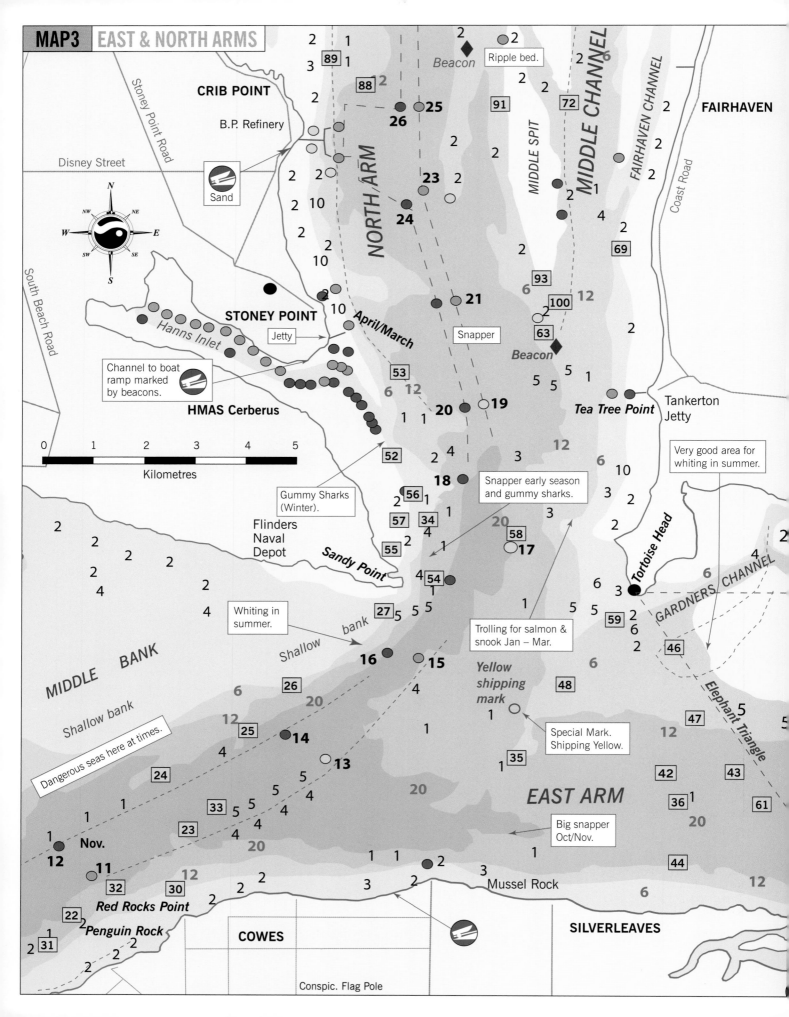

MAP3 EAST & NORTH ARMS

GPS MARKS FOR MAP 3 EAST & NORTH ARMS

22: PATRIC NEIDHART VENTNOR (SQUID AND WHITING)
S 38 27 432 E 145 11 018

23: ACE FISHING CHARTERS BUOY 11 (SNAPPER, APPROX. 21 M)
S 38 26 660 E 145 11 694

24: PATRIC NEIDHART BUOY 12 (GUMMIES WITH SQUID ON SLACK WATER)
S 38 26 321 E 145 11 589

25: REEL TIME CHARTERS BUOY 14 (GUMMIES YEAR ROUND)
S 38 25 613 E 145 13 056

26: PATRIC NEIDHART BUOY 14 (GUMMIES EBB TIDE)
S 38 25 477 E 145 13 286

27: JARROD DAY BUOY 16 (SNAPPER AUG–OCT, APPROX. 20 M)
S 38 25 063 E 145 13 793

30: TANKERS (WHITING)
S 38 26 811 E 145 12 817

31: EAST 7 (WHITING AND PINKIES)
S 38 27 068 E 145 11 722

32: LOW 11 (GUMMIES AND SNAPPER)
S 38 26 587 E 145 11 945

33: PATRIC NEIDHARDT BOUY 11 (SNAPPER)
S 38 27 086 E 145 10 803

34: REEL TIME CHARTERS BUOY 18 (PINKIES, SNAPPER, SMALL GUMMIES)
S 38 23 936 E 145 14 500

35: (SNAPPER, GUMMY AND SCHOOL SHARK)
S 38 25 758 E 145 15 207

36: (SNAPPER, GUMMY AND SCHOOL SHARK)
S 38 26 327 E 145 16 885

42: REEL TIME CHARTERS COWES
(GUMMIES, YEAR ROUND, SNAPPER SEPT– DEC, PINKIES DEC – APRIL)
S 38 26 177 E 145 16 792

43: ACE FISHING CHARTERS SILVER LEAVES
(MARK APPROX. 16 METRES)
S 38 26 135 E 145 17 169

44: COLIN GUILMARTIN SILVER LEAVES
(SNAPPER, EARLY SEASON, EBB TIDE, APPROX. 20 METRES)
S 38 26 504 E 145 16 719

46: ACE FISHING CHARTERS WHITING TORTOISE HEAD (APPROX. 2.5 METRES)
S 38 25 074 E 145 16 620

47: PENINSULA AND WESTERN PORT CHARTERS TORTOISE HEAD
(WHITING, JAN–MARCH, APPROX. 3.5 METRES)
S 38 25 438 E 145 16 737

48: REEL TIME CHARTERS TORTOISE HEAD (Whiting, salmon)
S 38 25 317 E 145 15 887

52: ACE FISHING CHARTERS HANNS INLET
(WHITING, APPROX. 11 METRES)
S 38 23 483 E 145 14 204

53: ACE FISHING CHARTERS HANNS INLET
(PINKIES AND WHITING, APPROX. 15 METRES)
S 38 23 185 E 145 14 548

54: REEL TIME CHARTERS SANDY POINT (GUMMY YEAR ROUND, SNAPPER SEPT–DEC, WHITING AND PINKIES DEC–APRIL)
S 38 24 509 E 145 14 303

55: PENINSULA AND WESTERN PORT CHARTERS (SANDY POINT WHITING AND PINKIES, NOV–MARCH, APPROX. 14.5 METRES)
S 38 24 346 E 145 14 333

56: WHITING
S 38 23 495 E 145 14 090

57: WHITING
S 38 23 697 E 145 14 150

58: BUOY 17 (DEEP WATER)
S 38 24 250 E 145 15 150

59: ELEPHANT MARK (ELEPHANT FISH)
S 38 24 770 E 145 16 510

61: TORTISE HEAD (SNAPPER)
S 38 26 268 E 145 16 450

63: SOUTH END OF MIDDLE SPIT
S 38 22 480 E 145 15 396

69: PENINSULA AND WESTERNPORT CHARTERS TANKERTON
(WHITING, NOV–MARCH, APPROX. 7.5 METRES)
S 38 21 850 E 145 16 041

72: EAST ENTRANCE TO THE CUT
S 38 20 905 E 145 15 582

88: ACE FISHING CHARTERS HASTINGS
(SNAPPER, EARLY SEASON, FLOOD AND EBB, APPROX. 17 METRES)
S 38 19 050 E 145 14 204

89: PENINSULA AND WESTERN PORT FISHING CHARTERS CRIB POINT
(WHITING, APRIL–MAY)
S 38 20 459 E 145 13 655

91: ACE FISHING CHARTERS MIDDLE SPIT (WHITING, SOUTH OF CUT)
S 38 21 080 E 145 14 965

93: ACE FISHING CHARTERS
(BOTTOM OF MIDDLE SPIT WHITING, APPROX. 2.5–6 METRES)
S 38 22 352 E 145 15 404

100: TANKETON (WHITING)
S 38 22 376 E 145 15 520

giving the angler a chance to physically see the ground they intend to fish when targeting whiting. The trick is to locate patches of sand interspersed within weed. By casting into them and then moving baits along the sand, whiting will come from the cover of the weed to hit the bait.

This channel is often used as a short cut by fishos who launch at Stony Point and fish the Corinella region.

BLAKES CHANNEL

This small narrow channel runs off Gardners Channel to follow the contour of the French Island shoreline. Whiting often feed at the entrance to Blakes Channel on the ebb tide. Flathead and salmon are often found in this area and the occasional elephant fish scares whiting fishos when it takes a pipi intended for a much smaller target. This is a great place to do some investigative fishing. You would be surprised how many big fish call a channel like Blakes home.

COWES

Cowes is the hub of Phillip Island and swells in holiday periods with people travelling from all over the State and the country to enjoy the pleasures that it has to offer. The options are endless as it is situated in a central position in relation to so many areas.

Cowes Pier is the only north facing pier in Western Port and is well known for its ability to produce every species that the Port has to offer.

Corinella, Rhyll, Tortoise Head, Stony Point and even the Nobbies are all within easy access. In saying this, I do not recommend using the boat ramp here. I prefer to travel to Rhyll.

Anglers heading down towards the open ocean at the Nobbies should be aware that a swell of 2–3 metres can often run though this area, especially on a south-westerly wind. This area can also chop up considerably when wind is blowing in the opposite direction to the tide.

There are plenty of good snapper, gummy shark and school shark marks within safe boating distance of Cowes. One particular area is around Buoy Marker 13. This is the beginning of McHaffies Reef and attracts a wide range of species including snapper, gummy shark, whiting and salmon. Work the tides and anchor accordingly.

Just out from the Cowes Pier is also productive for snapper and gummy shark. The bottom is quite muddy unless you anchor nearing the edge of the channel where there is some good reef.

Silver leaves

On the Phillip Island shore and situated between Observation Point and the Cowes Pier is a good stretch of water known as Silver Leaves. This area offers plenty of shelter from the hard southerly and south westerly winds. It is a slow, sloping bank with little tide and allows you to fish along this bank very close to shore in around 3–4 metres of water. This area is good for whiting and calamari and sees good numbers of school salmon at times. If you fish in around 20 metres of water off Silver Leaves early in the season you can encounter huge schools of snapper making their way up towards the Corals. During Late January, many snapper over the 20 lb mark have been caught along the edge of this bank. This area fishes best on the ebb tide, late in the evening.

Land Based fishing is also productive in the shallows. On the high tide, the sandy bank has deep divots which sees flathead hunt for minnows. Flicking soft plastics is effective.

Observation Point

Observation Point is the most northerly point on Phillip Island and is situated about 1–2 kilometres from the Rhyll Pier. Good catches of whiting and elephants are taken from the point close to shore while the tide is on the move. The deeper water between the point and Bird Rock on French Island produces every big fish that Western Port is famous for.

Boat ramps

Stony Point

This area has excellent launching facilities and for this reason it has become one of the most popular boat ramps on the Port. Due to its location it offers great access to the North Arm, the Cowes area, Western Entrance, Pt Leo and it is also frequented by offshore fishos heading toward Bass Strait for a days shark fishing. It can be found by travelling to the end of Stony Point Rd (Melway Ref 195 F5). Two ramps with a good gradient offer launching for most size craft on almost any tide.

Cowes

Cowes Boat Ramp is situated about 2 kilometres west of the Cowes Pier. Follow the main road from San Remo to Cowes and just prior to entering the township turn left at Church Street and follow this road for about 2 kilometres until turning right into Anderson Street. This ramp has a poor gradient, making it quite flat and hard to launch at low tide. The ramp is also very susceptible to northerly winds, so a stern rope can be handy to keep your craft aligned with the trailer whist launching and loading. The one bit of good news about this ramp…there is none. I would not recommend its use.

Land based fishing

Cowes Pier

Cowes Pier is very popular with holidaymakers and gets extremely busy at times, so you will have to be there early to reserve the best spot. It is found on The Esplanade at Cowes right in the middle of town (Melway Ref 634 D1). Some exceptional fish are taken here from time to time, with early morning and late evening to after dark the best times to fish. As this pier runs into deep water, it is very affected by tidal flow, so your trip should be planned with this in mind.

Barracouta, salmon, flathead, rock cod, snook, snapper, gummy shark and elephant fish are often caught at the end of the pier in the deep water. Fishing through the evening and into the dark on a moonlit night can produce anything. Thresher sharks to eight feet, big bronzies and other beasts that just can't be stopped inhabit this area over the summer months. Striped tuna and cured eel are the preferred baits.

Whiting and mullet are also taken from here particularly around halfway along the pier where the tide is not so strong. Lighter tackle can be used for these fish.

Stony Point Pier

Stony Point Pier offers plenty of variety due to its deep-water access and is found at the end of Stony Point rd (Melway Ref 195 F5). At the end of the day, there are not too many fish that you can't catch off it. The pier is famous for mullet, trevally, snook and big squid.

Massive seven gill sharks turn up from time to time but anglers are rarely geared up for the occasion. Gummy sharks are always a possibility with elephants ranging 2 – 4 kilos a big possibility between March and mid May. During the summer months, snapper are a common catch during the flood tides. Be careful of the channel markers as there is reef in the area and you can become snagged. Garfish are also quite a popular targeted species during the run out tide. Fish from the far left of the pier for best results. Berley is necessary.

Tankerton Pier

This pier offers some excellent fishing because it is harder to get to and therefore receives less angling pressure. It is located on French Island at the western end of Tankerton Rd at an area known as Tea Tree Point. Access is available via ferry from the mainland and many anglers choose to do all night sessions. Even though it is only about 3 metres deep, some very large fish are taken here. On the change of tide, this area can offer plenty of snapper and shark fishing, particularly at dusk or dawn. My late friend, Jeff Trembath first alerted us to the pier's outstanding fishing qualities when he took an 8.2 kilo snapper off this isolated structure. It is also a popular whiting haunt from December to March.

NORTH ARM

nglers travel from around the State to fish this area, and it was for me, the scene of my first serious Western Port fishing adventure. With first class launching facilities such as Hastings and good surrounds, the trip down is a very pleasant one. Warneet also offers quick access to the top of the North Arm for anglers from Cranbourne to the east.

The fishing in this area is excellent with every species available that the Port has to offer. From big snapper and gummies in the deeper channels to good numbers of whiting along the many drop-offs, this area really has something to offer every one. Famous 'hot spots' like Crawfish Rock, Long Reef, Lysaghts BP Jetty, Watson Inlet and the Middle Spit all call this area home. Unlike the top end of the Port, the water here is normally clean making fishing easy in most conditions.

WHERE TO FISH

CRAWFISH ROCK

Possibly one of the most well known landmarks in Western Port, the Rock is fully exposed at low tide and well disguised at high tide. It is a navigation hazard and must be avoided at all costs. Legend has it that it was originally known as Crayfish Rock by divers who used to pull crayfish from the many crevices, but the name slowly changed to Crawfish over a period of time. To this day anglers catch the odd crayfish on a pilchard intended for a snapper when fishing close to the rocky structure. In recent years, balmain bugs or Morton Bay Bugs as they are also known are also caught on occasion in this area. Being discarded from ships ballasts; they have set up residence and are quite abundant in the summer months.

Deep water surrounds the area and tidal flow is fast. This doesn't seem to bother the fish however. Every season Crawfish produces snapper over twenty pounds and some monster gummy sharks. November through March is prime snapper time at the Rock.

A sand spit extends to the west of the Rock. The edge of this spit produces good catches of snapper and whiting. When the tide slows anglers move in close to the rock to throw plastics into the rocks for trevally to a kilo.

QUAIL BANK

This area is one of the most underrated fisheries in the Port. Due to its protection from strong northerly winds, it is mainly only fished as a last resort and not a true destination. It is situated at the top of the North Arm spanning between Watson Inlet to the West and Rutherford Inlet (Warneet Channel) to the East. This bank travels for about 5 kilometres, parallel to the northern mainland shoreline, which gives great protection from those harsh northerly winds that normally occur each year in October and November. When this happens and you have already planned your fishing trip, this is usually the safest area to fish.

The Quail Bank itself is a slowly sloping bank that ranges from 2–5 metres over a distance of around 300 metres heading seaward before dropping over a shelf to 12 metres.

Good whiting are taken on the shelf in about 2–5 metres of water whilst the tide is running on either the ebb or flood. It is also a very good after dark location as big whiting move into the shallows for protection from predators. Just sneak out of one of the two channels that flank the bank and anchor in 1–2 metres of water.

When the tide slackens, it is the time to drop over the shelf into the deeper waters for larger whiting, good numbers of pinkies and big gummies. It is always worth having a big fish bait out the back when you target whiting, as you never know what will swim past.

Quail Bank is also one of the best locations to target and catch calamari year round. Fishing the flood tides is when most of the action occurs as calamari will be lurking around for easy prey. Drift fishing and casting artificial jigs is effective but this area also fished well for calamari when at anchor using baited jigs in a berley trail.

The Quail and Tyabb Banks produce quality calamari year round. Artificial jigs like this Ika are ideal.

Garfish can also be plentiful along the bank and tend to be up as shallow as 2 meters of water. Float fishing is the most effective technique.

WATSON INLET

This area has come a long way in recent years with a beautiful marina complex and restaurant situated on the eastern side of the inlet just south of the Yaringa Marine National Park. It offers boat storage, private launching for members, hire boats and a range of other related services. Call Yaringa Marina on 03 5977 4154 for more information.

The inlet has a deep channel that empties into the west end of Bagge Harbour at the top of the North Arm. Being situated at the most northerly point of the Quail Bank, it is clearly marked by port and starboard piles from the entrance to the marina, making it simple to navigate. It offers great fishing as well as giving full protection from those northerly winds previously mentioned. In more recent years this area has produced quality snapper and mulloway from September through January. It is also a popular whiting spot from December through April.

EAGLE ROCK

Leaving Watson Inlet behind and heading in a southerly direction for about 1.6 kilometres you will arrive at Eagle Rock, which is clearly marked with an Isolated Danger hazard beacon.

Although Eagle Rock does not protrude at low tide, it is advisable not to anchor within 50 metres.

Big fish still are caught here, but it has become a reliable pinkie snapper location with good numbers of fish in the 1–2.5 kilo vicinity turning up at different stages of the tide. Schools of fish tend to move through this area, hence it may produce one day and not the next. It can turn off and on like a switch, but it is always worth a look. It is not unusual to see as many as 20 to 50 boats on anchor here at the one time.

As the tide here runs at considerable strength, the time to fish

70: NORTH END OF MIDDLE SPIT
S 38 16 416 E 145 16 963

71: WEST ENTRANCE TO THE CUT
S 38 19 960 E 145 15 126

73: MOUTH OF WATSON INLET
S 38 15 703 E 145 15 672

74: EAGLE ROCK ISOLATED DANGER MARK
S 38 15 905 E 145 16 795

75: SCOTT HARPER (GUMMY SHARK, APPROX. 22 METRES)
S 38 15 811 E 145 17 489

76: REEL ADVENTURE CHARTERS
(EAGLE ROCK SNAPPER AND PINKIES, OCT–MARCH, APPROX. 19 METRES)
S 38 16 173 E 145 16 355

77: REEL ADVENTURE CHARTERS
(QUAIL BANK WHITING, DEC– FEB, APPROX. 3 METRES)
S 38 15 473 E 145 16 299

78: LYSAGHTS (SNAPPER)
S 38 17 350 E 145 14 900

79: CHRIS HALSTEAD LYSAGHTS
(SNAPPER, GOOD REEF AND CUNJE, APPROX. 14–15 METRES)
S 38 17 504 E 145 14 826

80: REEL TIME CHARTERS LYSAGHTS (SNAPPER, EARLY SEASON SEPT–NOV)
S 38 18 712 E 145 14 255

81: REEL TIME CHARTERS LYSAGHTS (SNAPPER, EARLY SEASON SEPT–NOV)
S 38 18 094 E 145 14 255

82: ACE FISHING CHARTERS LYSAGHTS
(SNAPPER, PINKIES FLOOD TIDE, APPROX. 14.5 METRES)
S 38 16 897 E 145 15 095

83: PENINSULA AND WESTERN PORT CHARTERS LYSAGHTS
(SNAPPER, OCT–NOV, APPROX. 14.5 METRES)
S 38 16 256 E 145 16 165

84: ACE FISHING CHARTERS LYSAGHTS
(SNAPPER, FLOOD TIDE, APPROX. 18 METRES)
S 38 17 407 E 145 14 807

85: PATRIC NEIDHART BUOY 29 (GUMMY, SNAPPER)
S38 18 712 E 145 14 302

86: BP (SNAPPER)
S 38 20 846 E 145 14 437

87: MOUTH OF HASTINGS CHANNEL
S 38 19 533 E 145 13 277

88: ACE FISHING CHARTERS HASTINGS
(SNAPPER, EARLY SEASON, FLOOD AND EBB, APPROX. 17 METRES)
S 38 19 050 E 145 14 204

89: PENINSULA AND WESTERN PORT FISHING CHARTERS CRIB POINT
(WHITING, APRIL–MAY)
S 38 20 459 E 145 13 655

90: ACE FISHING CHARTERS HASTINGS MIDDLE SPIT, (5–7 METRES AT LOW TIDE)
S 38 19 308 E 145 15 139

92: JARROD DAY MIDDLE SPIT (WHITING, ANY TIDE, APPROX. 2 METRES)
S 38 17 834 E 145 15 503

94: CRAWFISH ROCK (SNAPPER ALL ROUND)
S 38 16 200 E 145 17 850

95: TYABB BANK
S 38 16 400 E 145 15 600

96: HASTINGS (16 M SNAPPER)
S 38 19 188 E 145 14 030

97: MIDDLE CHANNEL (12 M SNAPPER)
S 38 19 216 E 145 16 352

98: MIDDLE CHANNEL (8 M SNAPPER AT END OF TIDE)
S 38 17 372 E 145 15 184

99: ESSO (REEF SNAPPER)
S 38 19 820 E 145 13 780

101: CRAWFISH ROCK BEACON
S 38 16 228 E 145 17 788

---

would be one hour each side of slack water. The ebb tide will flow much harder than the flood, so you will need to adjust your sinker weights accordingly.

Eagle rock is also renowned for salmon, pike and small tailor. Early morning and late afternoon appears to be the best feeding time for these particular fish. However, they can pop up any time of the day so it is always worth a look if you are in the area. The birds will be your best indication as to whether there are fish in the area feeding. When you notice this activity, it is worth trolling or casting into the school. Some of these salmon reach 2.5 kilos in weight and should never be underestimated as a quality light line sportfish. Always troll a deep diving lure in the spread with the chance of picking up a snook, pike, much bigger salmon or even a small kingfish. It is hard to go past a good salmon fillet for bait when there are good snapper in the area.

It pays to have a good look at a chart before fishing this area. There are plenty of great spots to fish if you know what you are looking for. On the southern side of Eagle amongst the rubble in 10 meters of water, big whiting are popular in season. Fish nearing a tide change for best results.

TYABB BANK

This area covers the slow slopping bank that spans between the Yarringa Harbour and the pier at Lysaghts. Like the Quail Bank, it has a very slowly sloping bank ranging from 3–12 metres over a distance of around 300–400 metres to seaward. Being almost 5 kilometres in length, it offers plenty of fishing space even on the busiest of days. Due to the gradual slope I find it best to fish in around 5–6 metres of water for whiting. Whiting feed on most of this ground, whilst big flathead, pike, salmon and garfish are also popular sport. It may take a few moves to find them, but when you do, berley will help to hold them at the boat.

Calamari are also a popular target nowadays especially one a high tide. Drifting is the preferred method while casting artificial jigs in a 3.0 size about the weed beds.

Moving out into deeper water on the edge of the Tyabb Bank will put you in with a chance off snapper to 6 kilos with September through December the best time. During these months whole squid heads (caught locally) fished on big snelled hook rigs will put you in with a chance to encounter that 20 pound snapper you have always dreamed of. Good gummies also call this area home.

EASTERN CHANNEL

Eastern Channel is situated almost directly south of Crawfish Rock and runs in a south south westerly direction very close to French Island along the majority of its western shoreline. It then empties into the Main Channel near Tankerton Pier. With French Island to the east side and the Middle Spit flanking the channel to the west, it makes the channel very stable with the tides running directly up or down with no cross-tides. It has a great deal to offer with little gutters running off the banks on either side. Fish at the mouth of these gutters on the ebb tide for best results on whiting

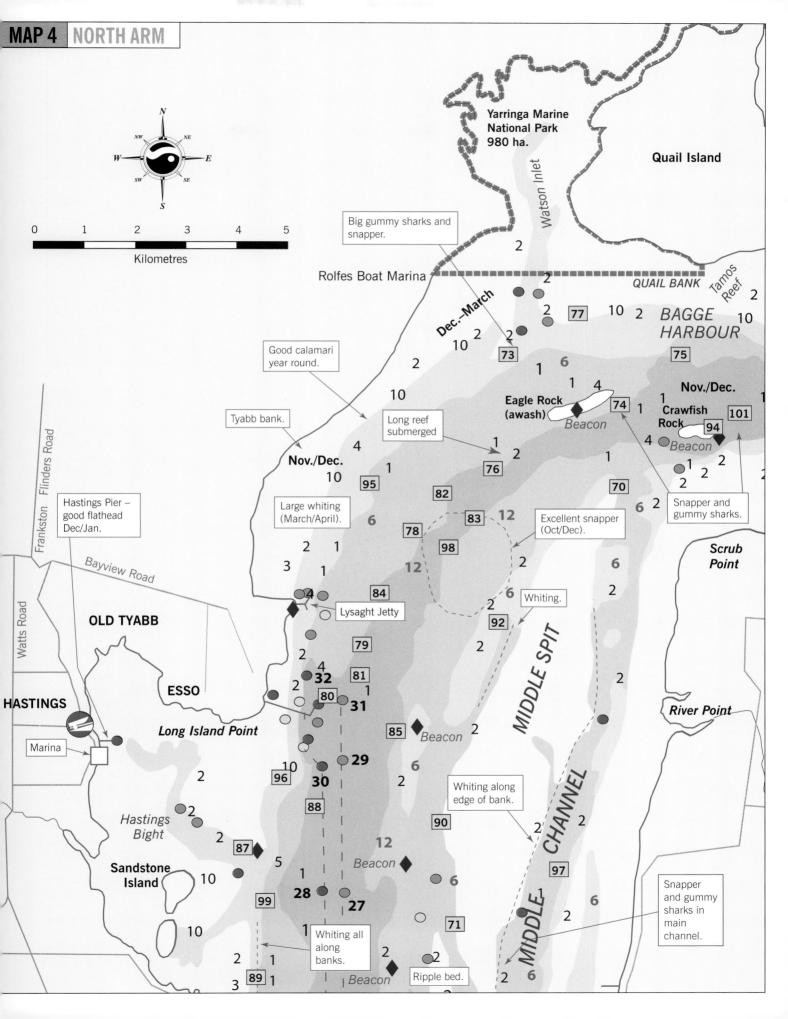

MAP 4 NORTH ARM

N
NW NE
W E
SW SE
S

0 1 2 3 4 5
Kilometres

Yarringa Marine
National Park
980 ha.

Quail Island

Big gummy sharks and
snapper.

Rolfes Boat Marina

Watson Inlet

QUAIL BANK

Tamos Reef

2

2

2

Dec.-March

10 2

2

2

10

BAGGE
HARBOUR

77

10 2

75

10

Good calamari
year round.

2

10

1 6

Long reef
submerged

Eagle Rock
(awash)

Beacon

74 1

Nov./Dec.

Crawfish
Rock

101

Tyabb bank.

Nov./Dec.

10

4

1

1

2

76

1

4

Beacon

94

2

2

Snapper and
gummy sharks.

95

2

1

2

70

Large whiting
(March/April).

82

6

83 12

98

Excellent snapper
(Oct/Dec).

6

Scrub
Point

78

12

Hastings Pier –
good flathead
Dec/Jan.

2 1

3 1

84

Lysaght Jetty

4

2

1

6

Whiting.

92

2

6

2

Frankston Flinders Road

Bayview Road

OLD TYABB

79

2

4

ESSO

81

2

32

1

Watts Road

HASTINGS

80

31

River Point

Marina

Long Island Point

85

Beacon

2

6

Middle Spit

2

10

29

2

96

30

Whiting along
edge of bank.

Hastings
Bight

2

88

90

2

12

Sandstone
Island

87

Beacon

6

5

97

10

6

Snapper
and gummy
sharks in
main
channel.

99

28

27

6

2

71

MIDDLE CHANNEL

10

1

Whiting all
along
banks.

2 1

2

2

89 1

Beacon

Ripple bed.

2

2

6

and fish over small mounds or humps on the bottom for pinkies.

At the top of the channel on the eastern side is a shallow bank signified by a green channel marker. The bank is around 3m deep on a low tide and fished very well for whiting during the ebb tide.

Moving south, the edges of the bank are full of weed in which calamari can be caught. Fishing the last two hours of the ebb tide and drifting along the edge of the bank is effective. Cast towards the banks edge and work your jigs fast. Size 2.5 and 3.0 jigs will see most of the action.

RED BILL CREEK

This creek is actually a little gutter that runs off French Island into the Eastern Channel almost opposite the Esso Refinery at Hastings. If travelling past, it is always worth a stop. King George whiting, grass whiting and leatherjackets normally feed here on the first of the flood and last of the ebb tides.

There is also a deep hole situated in the middle of the Eastern Channel at the mouth of the Red Bill Creek. This area has been kept quiet for too long by local Warneet anglers who take snapper to 10 kilos and gummies in excess of 25 kilos. It is worth having a good sound around this area to see what you can pick up.

MIDDLE SPIT

To the west of the Middle Spit is the Main Channel or more correctly, the North Arm. The shipping channel is marked by port and starboard buoys and anchoring is not permitted between these buoys, however there are still plenty of great fishing opportunities between the channel and the Spit.

As with the Western Entrance, some anglers now choose to drift with the tide until they find the fish. This has been very effective in recent seasons.

This must be one of the heaviest fished deep water locations on the Port. Some of my favourite and most consistent snapper marks lie in this body of water.

If you are unsure you can always anchor on the edge of the channel by lining up the shipping channel markers with the naked eye. Both buoy's 25 and 28 have a great reputation for producing snapper when fished in this fashion. Just plan to fish about 1–2 hours either side of the tide. I have had best success fishing the North Arm on the low tide change, but in saying that, the biggest snapper I have landed there was on a high tide change.

When the snapper are schooling from September to December it is not unusual to come across makos, threshers, bronze whalers and even white sharks from Stony Point to Eagle Rock.

Fish for whiting along the edge of the Middle Spit in 3–6 metres of water. Just make short moves up and down the bank. If you don't do any good within ten minutes, just move on. Keep the noise down and don't let the anchor chain slap on the side of the boat. Whiting are timid and will spook easily. Good quality whiting are caught along this spit on either tide. As the tide here will not be fast, fishing can be carried out for most of the day.

SUNKEN ISLAND

On the eastern side of the North Arm a green channel marker marks Sunken Island, a small sand bar covered by water both low and high tides. Whiting can be caught around it but it is the catches of garfish that raise eyebrows. Fishing in spring is when the larger models are caught and it is common to catch them as long as 50cm. A surface berley trail of pollard mixed with tuna oil works well. Baits should be suspended under a float setup.

THE CUT

This small channel runs between the Main and Eastern Channels starting almost in front of Esso Refinery. It cuts through the Middle Spit in a south easterly direction before emptying into the Eastern Channel.

Good whiting can be taken in this channel, but it generally produces small school size fish. Try fishing just outside the Eastern Entrance to this channel where a group of small underwater islands

lie. If you anchor between these islands you will possibly catch a feed of quality whiting.

SPRING CHANNEL

This channel is situated towards the southern end of the Eastern Channel and runs in a northerly direction very close to French Island for about 1 kilometre and passes the old Fairhaven Jetty. For this reason it is sometimes called the Fairhaven Channel

It is possibly one of the first channels to carry whiting early in the season and is always worth a look as it is a good sheltered channel with fishing possible on either tide. Whiting are also easy to locate, as the channel is not very wide and not all that deep. A little berley will help your situation immensely in this area.

HASTINGS CHANNEL

This is a long, winding channel that takes boat owners from the Hastings launching facility all the way to the North Arm. It is fairly well marked by port and starboard piles and although it is easy to follow the channel and navigate, many anglers end up on the mud trying to find a short cut or just by making a mistake. I always say that, 'there are only two types of anglers on Western Port, those that have run aground and those who will.' I came unstuck big time in this channel in 1991. If you look closely at the muddy bank you can still see the channel that my 140 hp Johnson forged through the mud as I hit it at warp speed. Worsteling's Channel, and what a beauty it was. Nothing that slopping around in the mud up to my 'Christmas crackers' didn't fix. A lot of pushing and we were on our way again.

Even though the channel takes a long time to navigate, it is worth the pain simply for the privilege of using the Hastings facilities.

You will often see anglers fishing around the mouth of the Hastings Channel and while you many think nothing can be caught here, whiting are the target. Often they are in good numbers, especial along the southern side.

SANDSTONE ISLAND

This sand cay is situated on the shoreline between the entrance to the Hastings Channel and the BP Refinery Jetty. From September through to December it produces monster calamari with squid available here until May. Squid to 4 kilos are a real possibility with 2.5 kilo squid hardly raising an eyebrow with the locals. The last hour of the ebb and the first hour of the flood are most productive as this exposes the sand spit and helps with positioning. Best results take place in 2–2.5 metres of water. Drifting is an option if weather conditions suit, but anchoring with constant moves tends to be more effective. This is a good place to fish between tides when the water is running too hard in the deep.

BOAT RAMPS

In my opinion, Hastings has the most modern and best boat ramp and parking area around the Port. A four lane concrete ramp and large floating pontoon makes launching quick and easy. A well-dredged approach to the ramp allows loading or launching at all stages of the tide. Be very careful on low water when walking on the ramps as green slime makes them extremely slippery and I have seen plenty of people including myself going for a sixer. This is no way to start or end a day on the water.

Parking for both cars and trailers is plentiful, providing the angler with all facilities for any sized craft. The new ticket machine for ramp fees only takes coins, so keep heaps of change handy.

SHORE BASED FISHING

HASTINGS PIER

Hastings Pier (Melways Ref 154 K11) is situated off Skinner St, Hastings and has plenty to offer the land based enthusiast. Most commonly caught species include salmon, whiting, mullet, silver trevally and flathead. Mulloway are an option if you are prepared to put in the effort and long hours. Try fishing over a tide change and don't forget the berley, as it will make the difference.

THE TOP END

This is undoubtedly one of my favourite areas on Western Port. It is so diverse and presents so many options for the thinking angler that one could fish a lifetime here and not even scratch the surface. I refer to this part of the Port as 'The Top End' of Western Port with most anglers finding access from Warneet, Tooradin and Blind Bight launching facilities. The long run to the fishing grounds tends to put the faint hearted off, which means more fish and fewer people for those prepared to give it a go.

The Top presents the angler with a wide range of diversities as an arterial-like expanse of channels wind their way from Crawfish Rock in the west towards Lang Lang in the east. There are very few channel markers in this area and anglers must read the surface action of the water or use a mapping GPS unit in an effort to distinguish shallow water from deep. If venturing out for the first time in these parts, you will need to take precautions and perhaps a friend who has some knowledge on the area.

The best and safest way would be to leave the boat ramp at either Tooradin or Warneet two hours before low tide and head down the channel keeping the red pile markers (port markers) on your right. At this level of the tide banks will be starting to appear and the channels becoming more prominent. If you do run aground, at least you will only have a relatively short wait before the tide begins to flood.

WHERE TO FISH

RUTHERFORD INLET (WARNEET CHANNEL)

This is a very busy channel as it is used by the local Yacht Club and anglers looking for access to the upper Port, thus making fishing difficult at times. If you are looking for a couple more fish to complete your bag or if you get blown out, this channel is always worth a look. King George whiting, grass whiting, mullet and silver trevally can be taken here but it is very hit and miss. Big flathead are sometimes taken on lures cast from small boats on the drift and big mulloway frequent this channel but are rarely taken by boaties. For some reason, the big jews tend to be hooked by land based anglers 90 per cent of the time. Sadly for land based anglers, these monsters are lost 95 per cent of the time!

This channel has some real potential for anglers fishing between the South Pier and the Ski Beach at Cannon Creek. This area holds flathead to 6 kilos, which will take plastics readily. Even though I am yet to see the proof, I have also heard reports of estuary perch coming from within the mangroves.

GENTLE ANNIE

This channel is unique in that it is within close proximity to anglers launching from Tooradin, Warneet and of course Blind Bight, yet it receives very little angling pressure when compared directly to similar locations. It is located between the Tooradin and Warneet channels and produces good fishing throughout the season with October to April the best months. It is a quiet little channel that starts at the beacon, known as the Basket before winding its way towards the Blind Bight jetty and boat ramp and the town itself.

This area can be fished in almost any tides or winds and occasionally produces a few surprises like seven gill sharks to 80 kilos and snapper to 8 kilos. Most of the whiting in this channel are small school fish early in the season, so be sure to put them on the ruler before keeping them for a feed. At the mouth of Gentle Annie near the Basket Beacon, a deep hole appears that usually carries big fish. It is a very popular snapper spot for the keen snapper angler, with the prime times always around the change of tide. Heading up the channel towards Blind Bight about 100 metres from the mouth to your left is Chainmans Creek. This tiny inlet drains water from the east of Chainmans Island and produces good numbers of smaller whiting, leatherjackets and big yellow eye mullet. This drain can be fished on both tides. An established berley trail will work wonders and attract a wide range of species to the area.

TOORADIN CHANNEL

Tooradin Channel is possibly the longest channel in Western

The Warneet channel or Rutherford Inlet as it is known is an impressive waterway with many hidden gems. Calamari, salmon, whiting, mulloway and estuary perch are a common catch throughout the year.

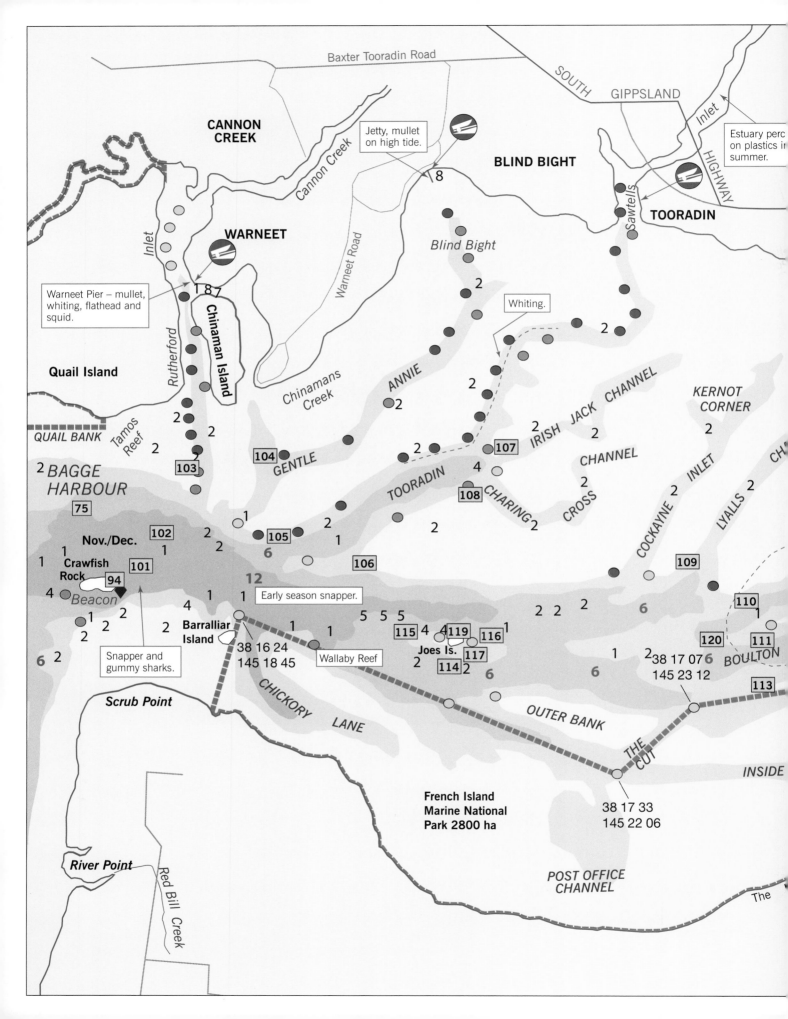

Baxter Tooradin Road

CANNON CREEK

Cannon Creek

BLIND BIGHT

SOUTH GIPPSLAND Inlet

HIGHWAY

Jetty, mullet on high tide.

8

Estuary perc on plastics in summer.

WARNEET

Sawtells

TOORADIN

Blind Bight

Warneet Road

Warneet Pier – mullet, whiting, flathead and squid.

1 8 7

Chinaman Island

2

2

Rutherford

Inlet

Chinamans Creek

Whiting.

2

Quail Island

Tamos Reef

2

2

ANNIE

2

KERNOT CORNER

2

2 *IRISH JACK CHANNEL*

2

QUAIL BANK

2

2

103

104

GENTLE

2

TOORADIN

2

107

CHANNEL

CROSS

2

2

2 **BAGGE HARBOUR**

75

108

CHARING

4

2

COCKAYNE INLET

2

LYALLS

2

CH

102

2

2

1

105

2

6

1

106

2

109

Nov./Dec.

1

101

12

Early season snapper.

110

1

Crawfish Rock

1

4

94

Beacon

4

2

2

1

5 5 5

2 2 2

6

120

111

2

1

2

2

1

115 4 4 **119**

116 1

2 38 17 07

6 **BOULTON**

6

1

2

2

Barralliar Island

Joes Is.

117

145 23 12

4

2

Snapper and gummy sharks.

38 16 24

145 18 45

Wallaby Reef

1

114 2

2

6

1

6

113

2

6 2

Scrub Point

CHICKORY LANE

OUTER BANK

THE CUT

INSIDE

38 17 33

145 22 06

River Point

Red Bill Creek

French Island Marine National Park 2800 ha

POST OFFICE CHANNEL

The

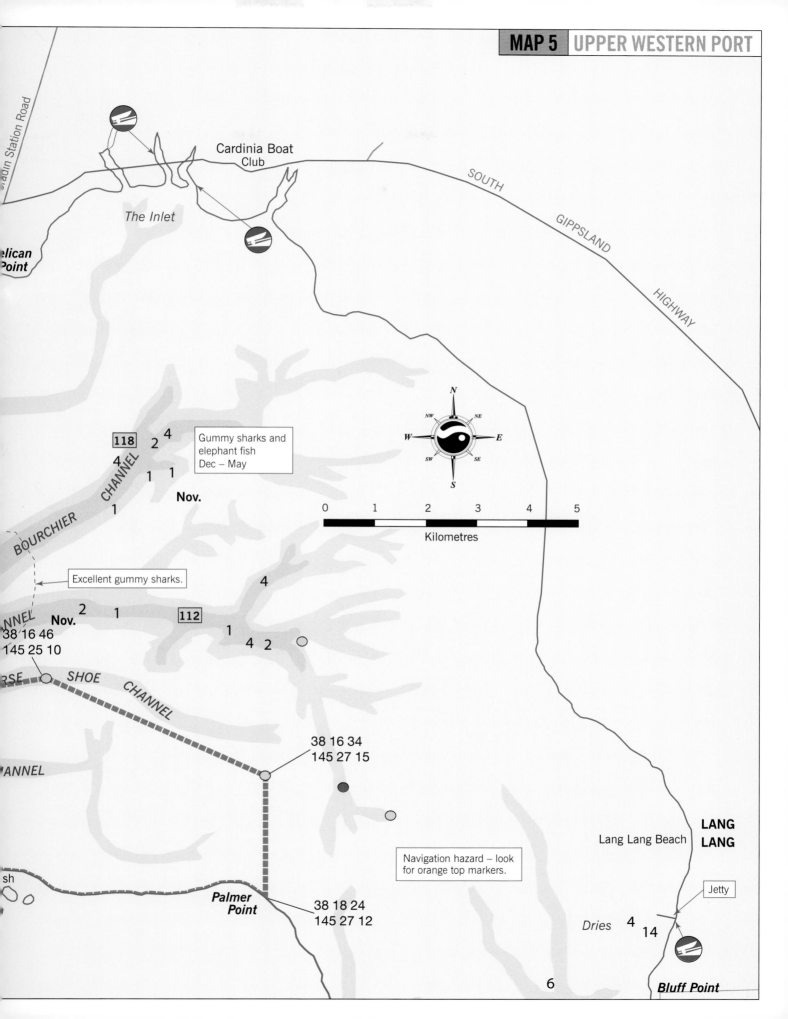

MAP 5 UPPER WESTERN PORT

Cardinia Boat
Club

SOUTH

GIPPSLAND

HIGHWAY

The Inlet

elican
Point

118 2 4

4
CHANNEL

1 1

Gummy sharks and
elephant fish
Dec – May

Nov.

1

BOURCHIER

Excellent gummy sharks.

4

NNEL 2 1 **112**

Nov. 1

38 16 46 4 2

145 25 10

RSE SHOE CHANNEL

ANNEL

38 16 34

145 27 15

LANG

LANG

Lang Lang Beach

Navigation hazard – look
for orange top markers.

Jetty

Palmer
Point

38 18 24

145 27 12

Dries 4 14

sh

N
NW NE
W E
SW SE
S

0 1 2 3 4 5

Kilometres

6

Bluff Point

GPS MARKS FOR MAP 5 UPPER WESTERN PORT

75: SCOTT HARPER (GUMMY SHARK, APPROX. 22 METRES)
S 38 15 811 E 145 17 489

94: CRAWFISH ROCK (SNAPPER ALL ROUND)
S 38 16 200 E 145 17 850

101: CRAWFISH ROCK BEACON
S 38 16 228 E 145 17 788

102: PETER FERGUSON CRAWFISH ROCK
(SNAPPER AND SCHOOL SHARK, NOV–DEC, APPROX. 21 METRES)
S 38 15 931 E 145 18 242

103: MOUTH OF WARNEET CHANNEL
S 38 15 595 E 145 18 486

104: MOUTH OF CHAINMANS CREEK
S 3815 251 E 145 19 076

105: MOUTH OF TOORADIN CHANNEL
S 38 15 914 E 145 19 404

106: PETER FERGUSON'S BROWNS RESERVE
(GUMMIES AND SNAPPER, FEB–MARCH
APPROX. 8 METRES, LAST TWO HOURS EBB AND FIRST HOUR FLOOD)
S 38 16 091 E 145 19 703

107: MOUTH OF IRISH JACK CHANNEL
S 38 15 162 E 145 21 208

108: MOUTH OF CHARING CROSS CHANNEL
S 38 15 227 E 145 21 181

109: MOUTH OF LYALL'S CHANNEL
S 38 16 185 E 145 23 104

110: MOUTH OF BOUCHIER CHANNEL
S 38 16 434 E145 23 588

111: MOUTH OF BOULTON CHANNEL
S 38 16 580 E 145 24 072

112: BOULTON CHANNEL (SNAPPER AND GUMMY)
S 38 16 201 E 145 25 924

113: MOUTH OF HORSESHOE CHANNEL
S 38 17 014 E145 23 606

114: (SNAPPER, GUMMY WHALER, SEVEN GILL)
S 38 17 091 E 145 21 121

115: WEST CARDINAL MARK, JOES ISLAND
S 38 16 557 E 145 20 711

116: EAST CARDINAL MARK, JOES ISLAND
S 38 16 632 E 145 21 121

117: REEL TIME CHARTERS JOES ISLAND
(GUMMIES WINTER MONTHS, APPROX. 17 METRES)
S 38 16 807 E 145 20 850

118: BOUCHIER GUMMY/SCHOOL SHARK
(BEST ON THE FIRST TWO HOURS OF THE EBB)
S 38 15 227 E 145 25 798

119: JOES ISLAND (7–10 M SNAPPER ALL ROUND)
S 38 16 600 E 145 21 100

120: BOLTONS (CHANNEL JUNCTION)
S 38 16 450 E 145 23 550

Port and is a very productive one. It is well marked with port and starboard piles and winds for about 10 kilometres in a southwesterly direction.

Whiting will start to appear from early November through until mid April and into May if the first frosts are late.

A lot of little gutters like Mugs Hole, Nagles Gutter and Golden Point empty into this channel on the last of the ebb tide washing food off the banks to waiting predators. When you arrive at one of these gutters, anchor at the mouth and fish will usually be feeding there. Whiting and flathead are the most likely fish to be taken at these spots, however the odd mullet, salmon and leatherjacket do appear at times.

Halfway along the Tooradin Channel at Port Beacon No. 12 and just below Nagles Gutter, two more channels join up. They are Irish Jacks and Charing Cross channels and both produce good fishing for whiting and the occasional gummy shark through the season. Whiting are usually found in big numbers here and it is common for anglers to fish for snapper and gummy shark at the same time. This is achieved by casting a snapper bait well clear of your boat, leaving your whiting lines clear of tangles. I have also hooked some big whaler sharks doing this and seen whalers to 100 kilos plus cruising in the shallows here.

An area known as Golden Point can be found at Port Beacon No. 10 on the east side of the channel, and is possibly one of the best known whiting marks in the Tooradin Channel. This mark will produce big whiting on both tides. On the starboard side of the channel, heading to sea between Golden Point and the mouth of the channel you will notice a stone bank, which is among the highest in the Port. Try

fishing the edge of this bank for quality whiting on most tides and good snapper at times.

If you are looking for quality whiting rather than quantity, try moving out to the middle of the channel at any point along its length when the tide begins to back off. This will often result in whiting in the 500–700 gram range, which are quality fish in anyone's book. It is important to remember that while the Tooradin Channel may be an arterial for boat traffic to gain access to the Port, but it is actually a very good fishery in its own right. The fish aren't aware of the fact that we use it as a thoroughfare, so it should not be overlooked.

JOES ISLAND

Situated, almost at the mid point between Crawfish Rock and the entrance to the Boulton channel is a sand spit known as Joes Island. It is distinguished by west and east cardinal marks at its extremities. Even though the word island conjures up ideas of vegetation, it is nothing more than a sand bar. This often confuses people who move on in search of an 'island'.

The fishing options around Joes will only be limited by your imagination. It is an excellent area for whiting with anglers concentrating in 4–11 metres of water. Bigger fish are normally taken here and it is quite common for whiting in the 45–50 cm bracket to take whole pilchards and squid aimed at much larger species.

Both small and large snapper frequent the area with fish to 6 kilos a common catch throughout the season. In March and April it is common to find large numbers of 27–45 cm snapper on one of Joes many drop-offs. Joes is also a good place to look for those early season reds, with September and October very productive.

When the tide floods or abates, an eddy forms at the ends of each side of the Island. Often, schools of silver trevally can be caught in them along with whiting and snapper in season.

What Joes is really famous for is its shark population. From gummies to whalers to seven gills—this area has them all. It will pay to do some prospecting in the area and remember that people say they caught fish at 'Joes' even if they are a kilometre from the island, so it does pay to look around. If you want a big shark, you should berley and use large baits. If you give it a red hot go, I think you will be surprised with the results.

CHANNELS AT THE TOP END OF THE PORT

If you are brave enough to venture east past Joes Island you will come across a host of channels that dominate the landscape of the north east corner of Western Port.

These channels are Cockayne, Lyalls, Bouchier, Boulton and Horseshoe.

Each channel is marked by a spit beacon and they produce a good variety of fish throughout the fishing season from September to May. Whiting, snapper, gummy shark, elephants, trevally, mullet and flathead are the most common fish that these channels produce. Big sharks, such as bronzies to 3.6 metres, seven gills over 100 kilos and others too scary to mention also frequent this area. You are also sure to encounter some monster rays, so make sure you take some serious tackle and heavy braid to slow them down.

COCKAYNE AND LYALLS

These areas receive little to no angling pressure except for keen whiting fishos who have their secret little spots that work on certain stages of the tide. The bank between the Tooradin Channel and Cockayne Channel is known as Browns Reserve and is a top whiting spot from January onwards. Anglers often work this bank and slowly leap frog their way from the mouth of the channel at Tooradin, along Browns Reserve and up the western bank of Cockayne. These channels also produce trevally, salmon and mullet in good numbers. Time spent flicking a large soft plastic will often result in flathead to a kilo with fish to 3 kilos a real chance. You can catch gummy shark here but from experience, they tend to be on the smaller side.

BOUCHIER CHANNEL

This channel receives even less attention than Boulton Channel but can be a real winner at times. After studying the charts and talking to people who have fished it for years, I managed to find some interesting geography that held some quality fish. Due to the fact that it is situated right next door to Boulton, they both hold similar species and can be fished in the same fashion.

You can move up and down the banks in search of whiting with fish over 40 cm common from February to May. They can be hard to find, but when you do get on to them be sure to hang on and have plenty of baits prepared.

Gummies and school sharks are the main target for those who make the long journey from Warneet and Tooradin. Find some of the deeper holes that do exist here, anchor up and sit tight. From February until April, Elephants are also a common catch and perform well when light tackle is used.

If you berley on the bottom with pellets and tuna oil you will be able to catch some fresh bait in the form of trevally and small salmon on slack water. Don't be scared to put a whole fish frame on a heavy outfit and keep your gimbal belt ready.

BOULTON CHANNEL

I have spent many hours over many years drowning baits in the Boulton. Even with the aid of navigation equipment most anglers are still terrified of this area and can't see the point of travelling so far. More fool them. If you line up the west and east cardinal marks on Joes Island and head east, north east for around 4–5 kilometres you will find yourself near the mouth of the Boulton. This channel is synonymous with snapper to 12 kilos (usually from march to June)

and good sizes and numbers of King George whiting. It is most famous however, for its large numbers of big gummy shark. As the tide ebbs the gummies swim off the banks and retreat into deeper water. If you position your boat in the right area you can literally fish ten square kilometres of the Port as the fish filter past your baits in a funnel-type effect. Some of the most productive locations are to anchor at the mouths of the smaller feeder channels which run into Boutlon. Start fishing an hour before high and stick it out all the way to low if you can. Even when the tide is belting past you are still in with a good show.

THE HORSESHOE

This channel is not clearly marked so care must be taken or you could spend some serious hours on the mud. Because of its location, tidal flow is usually fairly slow, especially on the flood tide, allowing fishing with light sinkers most of the time. Good catches of whiting are taken all along this gutter, only moving your boat a few metres at a time. Big trevally are also a regular visitor to this area along with seven gill sharks and whalers for those who want to put the time in. This channel is not renowned for snapper, even though it does produce some fish to around 3 kilos after Christmas.

BOAT RAMPS

Warneet, Blind Bight and Tooradin all have safe ramps, with the ramps at Warneet and Tooradin by far the best.

WARNEET

Warneet has two ramps which include the old ramp to the south and the newer of the two ramps, which has a much better gradient and a purpose built floating pontoon, to the North. This ramp has recently had an upgrade allowing a greater range of boats better launching. In saying that, the ramp is quite shallow and on a low tide, launching may be a non event. Where possible, launch a few hours surrounding the high tide and return around the same. They are located by following Warneet Rd to the end and then turning left into Kallara Rd which turns into Rutherford Parade (Melway Ref 142 E13). Both ramps can be used and some anglers choose to launch from the sand between the two when conditions are favourable. Even with the new ramp you will still have to launch around the tides with a low low tide causing some real problems. I have returned to the ramp late at night to find 5 metres of mud between the water and the ramp. You also have to watch the tide here as it runs across the ramp with vigour. On a flood tide you have to be careful not to be sucked under the pier, which runs parallel to the ramps, to the north side.

This is one of the most practical launching facilities on the Port as it is centrally located to the entire North Arm and The Top End. For this reason it is popular with smaller craft whose owners don't want to travel long distances over open water.

TOORADIN

The Tooradin Ramp has excellent triple launching facilities with a catwalk to the end of ramp and a floating pontoon. Tooradin also received an upgrade in 2013. The dual-lane boat ramp has been widened to three lanes and new floating pontoons have replaced old timber jetties. Follow the South Gippsland Highway to Tooradin and turn right as soon as you cross over the inlet. The ramp is located on the south side of the Highway (Melway Ref 144 A4). An hour each side of low water should be sufficient to load or unload your boat and the ramp should not be approached at low tide.

BLIND BIGHT

The Blind Bight Ramp dries out at low tide and around half tide is the safest time to approach it. It has a gradient of 1:11 and can be found off Anchorage Drive (Melway Ref 143 C10) It is usually only used by locals as it is too easy to be left high and dry.

Tidal Flow in Upper Western Port

This is an area where you can really use the tides to your advantage. The tides here are quite different to most other parts of the Port with a couple of reasons responsible for this. First, many creeks empty into the Port here, and on the ebb tide these creeks, plus the water running off the banks, build up the momentum of the tide. Second, it is just the opposite on the flood tide. As the tide floods, the water spreads itself over the banks giving it a greater area to flow, thus allowing the tide to slow right down. Remember this when planning your next trip and also take the wind conditions into account as they can speed up or slow down the tide. This is an extremely large body of water that is affected by winds from almost every direction.

Winds

As this part of the Port is open to wind with no immediate cover, one important factor needs to be studied carefully. The area is harshly subjected to easterly winds, so when they occur, it is almost impossible to fish. The reason is the lack of grass on the banks, which causes the mud to be washed off on the low tide making the water dirty. Remember that fish aren't always keen to feed in dirty water, but at the same time I have caught some beautiful gummies and snapper in water conditions that could best be described as pea soup.

SHORE BASED FISHING

Both the Tooradin and Warneet foreshores offer a good day for the family with fine amenities including barbecues, playgrounds and picnic areas. Activities include swimming, beach cricket and of course, good fishing.

Warneet Pier

Warneet has two piers. One at the boat ramp and another about a kilometre up the Rutherford inlet toward Cannons Creek. The main pier is situated on Rutherford Parade (Melway Ref 142 E11) and runs parallel to the boat ramp across the inlet. This is an extremely popular land based haunt that usually produces a fish for anglers who put the effort in. Species available include whiting, mullet, salmon, pike, trevally, flathead, calamari, mulloway and toadfish by the dozen.

A small channel makes its way under the pier about half way along the structure. Check it out at low tide and then go back on the flood for a good chance of whiting and mullet.

The key here is to berley with pellets and tuna oil in a cage on the bottom and then fish your paternoster rig near the cage, but downstream of the tidal flow. Throughout the summer months, schools of silver trevally swarm into Rutherford Inlet and are a common catch from the pier. Trevally range from 15cm to 50cm and can be a real handful to land. Calamari have been increasing in numbers over the past few years. They are common year round and respond well to size 2.0 and 2.5 artificial jigs.

Bass yabbies can be pumped at the base of the pier with the north jetty normally more productive. On the low tide the mud is soft; always pump for yabbies on a mid tide. Small mullet can be caught for live baiting for big mulloway, which also frequent this area. Cast baits towards boat moorings for best success and fish a couple of days either side of the full moon from January to April.

Tooradin Inlet

The Tooradin foreshore (Melway Ref 144 A3) is very special to me as it was the scene of my very first Western Port fishing experience. When I was in grade 5, a mate and I convinced his mum to take us down to Tooradin to catch a fish. We fished near the boat ramp and caught zip. The fact of the matter is that we still had a ball and I have had plenty of good days there since. There are lots of good fishing options here with hundreds of metres of accessible shoreline both sides of the highway.

There is also a good little pier with a lower landing to help with closer access to the water on low tide. Bay trout (small salmon) and mullet are the most common fish caught, although the odd whiting, estuary perch and mulloway are taken from time to time. These fish appear to remain in this inlet all year round, so if the weather is fine at any time of the year, a trip down may be worthwhile. Remember to plan your trip around a high tide.

Best baits include pipis, mussels and pilchard fillet. The toads tend to leave the pillie alone a little longer. When fishing with young children, boredom can set in quick if there is little action. Float fishing makes it much more enjoyable as children can watch it bob up and down while the smaller fish are picking at the bait. When it does go under, their excitement is uncontrollable.

Deep and Cardinia Creeks

These two channels which drain water from the Koo Wee Rup swamplands into the upper reaches of Western Port may look very average, but they do produce some good to excellent fishing at times. It is almost impossible to drive down the South Gippsland Highway over Deep Creek (Melway Ref 612 Q8) or Cardinia Creek (Melway Ref 612 Q8) without seeing someone wetting a line.

You will have to fish over the high tide as there is very little water in either at low. Mullet are the main target with fish to 50 cm taken at times. Estuary perch to 2 kilos are also a pleasant surprise with dusk the best time to target them. If you like exploring, follow the creeks up stream. There is plenty of good habitat that receives very little angling pressure.

LEFT: The Warneet pier is popular amongst anglers when targeting calamari. Mulloway are also targeted but many anglers get busted off on the nearby channel markers and boat moorings.

CORINELLA AND SURROUNDS

Tidal movement can be huge in the Port. The Corinella Pier photographed at low tide shows just how much it can drop.

ocal anglers from Corinella, Grantville, Coronet Bay and Lang Lang recognise this area as the prime fishing area of Western Port. They used to have it to themselves, but then the elephants and mulloway turned up and news got out.

In the last two decades this area has gone from one of the quietest, to one of the busiest on the Port. When the elephants are on and the weather is good, boat ramp queues can see up to a three hour wait. The fishing is so good that people don't seem to mind.

This area also offers access to Lang Lang and surrounding waters. Very few people make a right hand turn at the end of the Corinella Channel, so even on the busiest of days you can find a place of your very own somewhere.

WHERE TO FISH

The channel from Corinella only travels for about 500 metres before emptying into the Main Channel marked at the entrance by a red intermittent flashing beacon. Be careful navigating as it is not clearly marked and some people have got into a bit of trouble cutting the corner on the inside of the dogleg. After arriving at the mouth of the channel, if you turn right (in a northerly direction) you can follow the edge of the bank towards Guys Channel. Good catches of whiting are taken all along this bank fishing in 3–5 metres of water. This is also a great area to fish for live bait for mulloway and snapper. A little berley will usually attract a good school of mullet and small salmon. Keep working along this bank and you will arrive at Guys Channel.

GUYS CHANNEL

This area does produce some surprisingly good fish at times. If you anchor at the mouth of the channel on the ebb tide you can find some good sized whiting as they feed on the run-off. This channel heads towards the mainland, so if you intend investigate it, travel slowly as it is very shallow and winds quite sharply. Bigger fish such as elephants, pinkies and jewfish also frequent this area, especially after dark. The mouth is the best place to find them on the ebb tide with any area along the channel, but towards the end, good

for gummies and mulloway on the flood. Using berley is a sure way to get the fish fire up. A pot filled with pellets and pilchard left to rest on the bottom will work extremely well. Fish your baits in the trail and hold on.

TENBY CHANNEL

A further 1 kilometre north east past the entrance to Guys Channel and still following the eastern edge of the bank, you come across Tenby Channel. This is a relatively small channel that winds its way to the mainland at Tenby Point. This is not traditionally a good whiting spot, but it is always worth a quick look as not many anglers target this species here.

Anglers launching from Grantville can fish these waters but must realise limited time is available as the tide in this area almost empties right out. Hence a lot of planning is needed. Half tide is required to either load or launch at the Grantville ramp, so if a trip were to be planned from Grantville, I suggest it be when the tide is flooding. This will give you around six hours fishing before arriving back at the ramp. This ramp has seen better days and there has been very little if no maintenance at all. Ideally, it would be best to launch at Corinella and head north to Tenby Channel.

Even though it is hard to believe, snapper to 23 pound (10.5 kilos) along with big gummies have been taken from the beach in this area in just a metre of water at night. For those keen to put in the time and effort, this location is also known for delivering some excellent catches of mulloway. Fishing around the mouth of the channel is very popular for snapper and school mulloway to 8 kilos. Fresh calamari baits are ideal.

LANG LANG

The top area of the Port, north of an imaginary line drawn between the Tenby Channel and Freeman's Pont, to Lang Lang, is relatively uncharted water as far as fishos are concerned. I know and or communicate with thousands of anglers who own boats, and would not know five who fish this area on a regular basis. To top that I probably couldn't find 25 that have fished it in the last year.

This is a sad state of affairs as the fishing potential here is

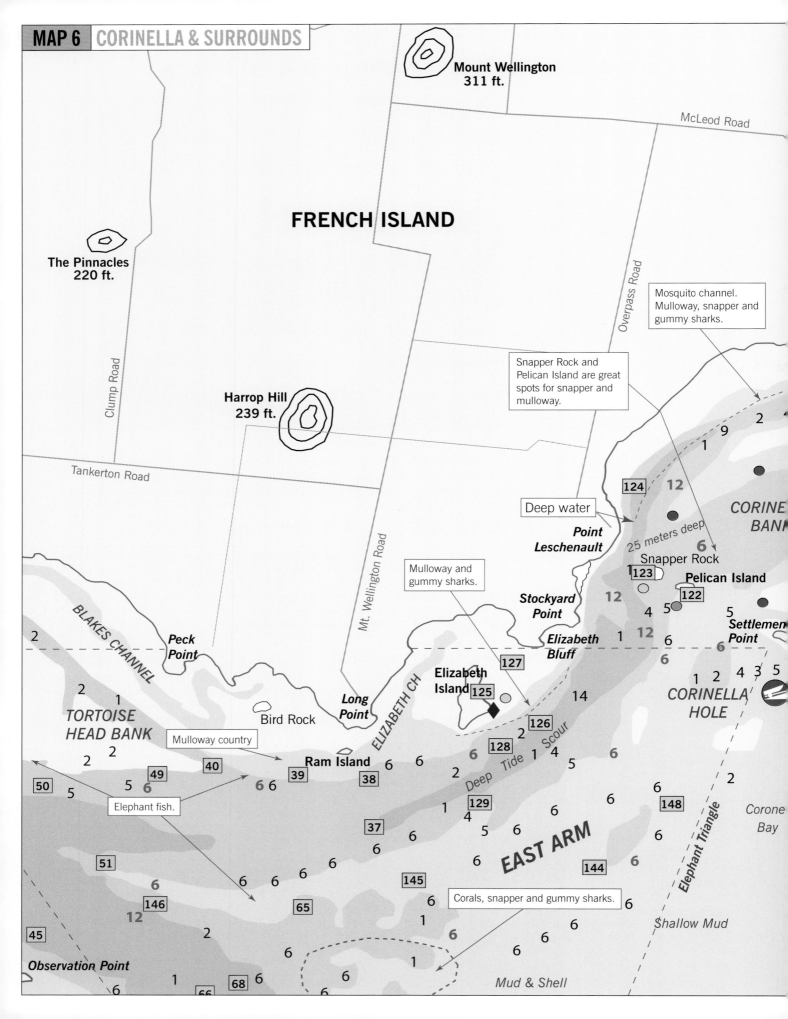

MAP 6 CORINELLA & SURROUNDS

Mount Wellington
311 ft.

McLeod Road

FRENCH ISLAND

The Pinnacles
220 ft.

Overpass Road

Mosquito channel.
Mulloway, snapper and
gummy sharks.

Snapper Rock and
Pelican Island are great
spots for snapper and
mulloway.

Clump Road

Harrop Hill
239 ft.

Tankerton Road

2

9

1

124 **12**

Deep water

CORINE
BANK

*Point
Leschenault*

25 meters deep

6

Snapper Rock

1 123

Pelican Island

Mulloway and
gummy sharks.

*Stockyard
Point*

12

122

4 5

5

*Settlemen
Point*

Mt. Wellington Road

*Elizabeth
Bluff*

1 **12**

6

6

5

*Peck
Point*

BLAKES CHANNEL

2

2 1

**TORTOISE
HEAD BANK**

2

Mulloway country

40

*Long
Point*

Bird Rock

ELIZABETH CH

*Elizabeth
Island* 125

127

126

14

Deep Tide Scour

2

1 4

5

**CORINELLA
HOLE**

2 1 4 3 5

5

2

50

5

49

6

39

Ram Island

38

6

6

2

6

128

2

1

6

6

148

Corone
Bay

Elephant fish.

5

6 6

2

6

1

129

4

6

6

6

6

6

51

37

9

6

EAST ARM

6

6

6

144

6

Elephant Triangle

6

146

6

65

145

6

1

6

6

6

12

2

6

6

Corals, snapper and gummy sharks.

6

1

6

Shallow Mud

45

Observation Point

1

66

68

6

6

Mud & Shell

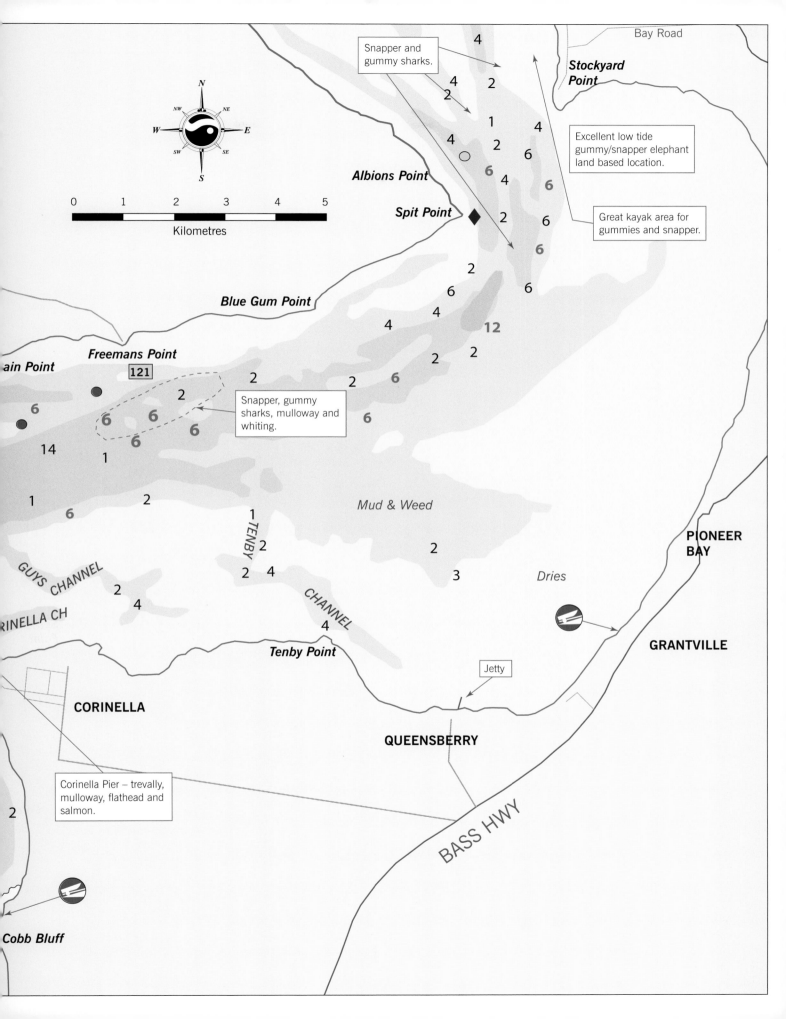

Bay Road

Stockyard Point

Snapper and gummy sharks.

4

4   2

2

1

4   2   4

4   6

Albions Point   6   6

Spit Point   ◆   2   6

2   6

6   6

12

4

Blue Gum Point   2   2

2

Freemans Point

121

2

●   2

6   6   6

●   6   6

14   6

1

1   2

6

1   *TENBY*

2   2

GUYS CHANNEL   4

2

RINELLA CH   4

CORINELLA

Tenby Point

QUEENSBERRY

Corinella Pier – trevally,
mulloway, flathead and
salmon.

2

Cobb Bluff

Excellent low tide
gummy/snapper elephant
land based location.

Great kayak area for
gummies and snapper.

Snapper, gummy
sharks, mulloway and
whiting.

Mud & Weed

2

3

Dries

PIONEER
BAY

GRANTVILLE

Jetty

BASS HWY

4   2

4

CHANNEL

4

GPS MARKS FOR MAP 6 CORINELLA AND SURROUNDS

37: RAM ISLAND (SNAPPER, GUMMY, ELEPHANT)

S 38 25 898 E 145 20 936

38: COLIN GUILMARTIN RAM ISLAND
(ELEPHANTS, MULLOWAY, APRIL–MAY, APPROX. 5M)

S 38 25 533 E 145 21 052

39: COLIN GUILMARTIN RAM IS/BIRD ROCK
(ELEPHANTS MARCH–MAY, SNAPPER EARLY SEASON, START OF FLOOD)

S 38 25 642 E 145 20 212

40: COLIN GUILMARTIN GARDNERS CHANNEL EXIT,
(ELEPHANTS, SNAPPER, GUMMIES, APPROX. 10M)

S 38 25 556 E 145 19 560

45: PENINSULA AND WESTERN PORT
(CHARTERS OBSERVATION POINT SNAPPER, NOV–MARCH)

S 38 26 898 E 145 18 338

49: COLIN GUILMARTIN TORTOISE HEAD BANK (SNAPPER, EARLY SEASON,
START OF FLOOD TIDE, GUMMY, SCHOOL SHARK, JAN–MARCH, ELEPHANTS)

S 38 25 703 E 145 19 147

50: COLIN GUILMARTIN TORTOISE HEAD BANK (SNAPPER, EARLY SEASON,
START OF FLOOD TIDE, GUMMY, SCHOOL SHARK, JAN–MARCH, ELEPHANTS)

S 38 25 689 E 145 17 995

51: COLIN GUILMARTIN EAST ARM
(BIG SNAPPER, GUMMY, SPRING AND SUMMER, APPROX. 9 METRES)

S 38 26 325 E 145 18 352

65: COLIN GUILMARTIN MIDDLE GROUND
(GUMMY, SCHOOL SHARK, PINKIES, 4–9 METRES)

S 38 26 882 E 145 21 186

68: COLIN GUILMARTIN CORALS (SNAPPER, GENERAL AREA)

S 38 27 150 E 145 20 550

121: FREEMAN'S POINT SHARK HOTSPOT

S 38 22 438 E 145 28 458

122: PELICAN ISLAND LANDMARK

S 38 24 293 E 145 24 340

123: SNAPPER ROCK LANDMARK

S 38 23 998 E 145 23 968

124: CORINELLA BARGE HOLE

S 38 23 633 E 145 23 789

125: ELIZABETH ISLAND LANDMARK

S 38 25 054 E 145 22 335

126: COLIN GUILMARTIN ELIZABETH ISLAND (GUMMIES, SNAPPER,
MULLOWAY, SCHOOL SHARK, 90 MIN EACH SIDE OF TIDE)

S 38 25 298 E 145 22 955

127: COLIN GUILMARTIN ELIZABETH BLUFF (ELEPHANTS, PROTECTED
FROM WESTERLY WINDS, APPROX. 8 METRES)

S 38 25 025 E 145 22 586

128: ELIZABETH ISLAND (HIGHLY PRODUCTIVE AREA – SNAPPER ALL ROUND)

S 38 25 200 E 145 22 600

129: COLIN GUILMARTIN ELIZABETH ISLAND (GUMMIES, SNAPPER)

S 38 25 968 E 145 21 785

144: CORONET BAY (6–16 M SNAPPER)

S 38 26 450 E 145 23 190

145: CENTRE TRIANGLE (ELEPHANT FISH)

S 38 26 625 E 145 21 129

148: CORONET BAY (SNAPPER MARK)

S 38 25 949 E 145 23 730

---

awesome. It is the home of gummy sharks and school sharks. Elephants also turn up here in late April and early May when they have gone quiet elsewhere.

Because the water is always dirty here, try baits with a good smell and scent like cured freshwater eel, striped tuna and fresh salmon or trevally fillets.

The great thing about this area is that there is lots of exploring to do and many great spots to discover. Study the charts and maps and with a little bit of imagination, you will soon find some real hot spots. Just follow your instincts and believe in yourself.

On a calm summer night, this can be a great place for an all nighter. With plenty of moon in the sky, the gummies and mulloway are always on the chew in shallow water.

MOSQUITO CHANNEL

This channel, which follows the shoreline of French Island very closely, has so much to offer anglers. It is very well protected from most winds and offers a host of species. Just a short run from Corinella, this area is very popular with smaller craft.

The Mosquito Channel can be found directly opposite the Corinella Light on the French Island side and starts just north of the barge landing before heading up towards Freeman's Point. This channel has become a mulloway Mecca in recent years with school fish in the 8–12 kilo range the norm. Fresh squid tends to be

the go for jewfish, but good fish are also landed on fish fillets and the humble old pillie. The channel is quite small and "mulloway hotspots" tend to be kept only to those that found them. One of the most popular locations is under the cliffs. Always fish the tide changes and moon phases. Mulloway are in their prime from December through to March.

Some quality snapper to 8 kilos also call this area home and it gets invaded with elephants from mid March onwards. This channel is full of undersized school sharks, yet big fish never seem to turn up here. The channel also produces whiting, flathead and mullet on both tides. The tidal flow is not too fast, allowing fishing through most tides without problems.

If you ever have a few spare hours you could do worse than to sound around this channel making some marks for future reference. The bottom is up and down all over the place and offers plenty of good holding and congregating areas for big fish.

FREEMAN'S POINT

At Freeman's Point, better known as the Old Prison Jetty, good catches of whiting are continually taken on the edges of the banks along with small jewfish to around 4 kilos.

The area holds a lot of shallow water, so if you approach, do so with caution. Once you have found the bank edge, continue to work along these edges towards Spit Point.

The area off Spit Point and through to Freeman's Point holds some big fish potential. The mariner's chart clearly indicates several huge underwater reef structures that produce everything from monster gummy sharks to snapper, 25 kilo mulloway and 3 metre seven gill sharks. The tide runs hard here so target your species two hours either side of the change.

A berley cage attached to your anchor will help to draw the fish to your baits. This area will always produce a real mixed bag.

PELICAN ISLAND

If you travel to the end of the Corinella Channel you will be able to see Pelican Island to your left. It is almost an extension of Settlement Point and is exposed at all stages of all tides. It is only a small island, but it has diverse fishing conditions on each of its sides. The deep water to the west sees snapper, gummies and elephants in the season, but the water runs hard.

On the east side of this island, (Settlement Pt side) there is a stretch of normally very rough water. This area is very susceptible to wind against tide conditions and can get very nasty with a short, sharp chop. I would avoid this area totally. There is also a large submerged reef just to the east. It is not pretty if you hit this.

On the south side of the island is a slowly, sloping rubbly bank that progressively drops to about 8 metres. As the ebb tide rushes past the island, a large eddy is formed where predators such as mulloway wait in ambush for disoriented baitfish such as salmon and mullet. This is a popular area for anglers to target mulloway with soft plastics. Fish to 4 kilos will hang out here from January to April.

SNAPPER ROCK

This rocky island is located between Pelican and French Islands. The deep water in this area also offers plenty of big fish. A lot of big snapper are taken around this rock (it didn't get its name for any other reason) throughout the season with the best tides being the first two hours of both the ebb and flood. It also produces monster mulloway in excess of 30 kilos, but with little or no consistency.

One of the deepest parts of Western Port is found between Snapper Rock and the barge on French Island. At around 36 metres, the Corinella Hole is one scary piece of water. Try to Anchor out of the hole and fish your baits back into it. You will have to choose your tides carefully as this area gives you a very narrow window of opportunity.

The Main Channel directly behind Snapper Rock heads in a south-westerly direction close to French Island, past Elizabeth Bluff and Elizabeth Island before emptying into the East Arm Channel at this point.

ELIZABETH ISLAND

This island is often hard to locate as it is camouflaged by French Island in its background. Deep water flanks the island's eastern shoreline and produces almost every species found in Western Port, dependent only on depth and time of year.

Past owner of the Kilcunda Caravan Park, Colin Guilmartin loved this area and had great success here. He had two great marks situated on the edge of the large tidal scour, which runs around the Island. Make sure you use your sounder to position yourself right on the edge of the bank. Even though the tide runs very hard, you should have about an hour and a half either side of the tide to target gummy sharks, school sharks, mulloway and

snapper. If you're partial to soaking big baits, do so here for bronze whaler sharks to 200 kilos.

A small channel known as the Elizabeth Channel winds its way behind the island with its entrance found to the south-west. Not often fished, it is well worth a look for whiting, elephant fish and mulloway.

CORONET BAY

Almost south-east off Corinella Point and around the bluff is Coronet Bay, a very productive whiting and garfish area for most of the season. As this is a slowly sloping bank without a really fast tide, fishing can continue for most of the day. It is an easy area to fish with a bit of prospecting normally producing rewards. Allow yourself fifteen minutes for the fish to pick up the bait and berley smell. If this time passes without success, move a short distance, and repeat this until you start to get results. The best fishing from this location will take place at night on a full moon. The whiting, mullet, gummies and even pinkies feed on the bank and are easy pickings for keen anglers.

Although it is best known for whiting, the odd leatherjacket, mullet and silver trevally are also caught. The sandy bottom also attracts fair quantities of good-sized flathead.

If you don't have a bait, don't worry as fishing from a kayak is very profitable. The carpark is only ten meters from the shoreline and you only have a short paddle to where the whiting can be caught.

This is also a very popular area for spotlighting garfish and flounder after dark.

Heading in a southerly direction and following the mainland shores towards Kennedy Pt, you will arrive at Reef Island. This area can be easily found as the island protrudes from the mainland. Good broken grounds (sand and weed patches) allow plenty of opportunities for good whiting, rock flathead leatherjackets and gars.

Mulloway and big snapper are also taken in this area after dark on live baits suspended about 75 per cent of water depth under a float.

If you move out onto the mud you will encounter bag limit quantities of elephants through March and April.

SHORE BASED FISHING

LANG LANG PIER

The Lang Lang pier for those that fished it, held a lot of history and many fishing stories to go with it. Storms and bad weather damaged the pier beyond repair and as a result it was torn down. For a period of time, few anglers fished from the beach but these day's it is one of the greatest land based gummy shark fishing locations around the Port.

RIGHT: Settlement Point with Snapper Rock and French Island in the distance is a top land based location during low tide. Snapper, whiting, silver trevally, elephants and gummy sharks can all be caught.

This area fish's best on a high tide as you'll only be casting into 1-2 meters of water. The area has a mud lined bottom. It is crutial that a high tide be fished as during a low tide, the area will be almost bone dry. There is very little by-catch here apart from the odd yellow eye mullet for those fishing light tackle and small baits. From February through to May, elephant sharks are also a common catch. Gummy sharks will take a wide range of baits but at this location, a favoured is a big juicy banana prawn. Local kayak anglers fish out from Lang Lang and have proven that banana prawns are the top bait. Other baits include squid, fish fillets, cured eel and pilchards.

STOCKYARD POINT

In my opinion, this is the best land based location on Western Port. It can be found (Melway Ref 612 R9) by turning off the Bass Highway down Bay Rd. If you walk out to the point and cast into the channel you are in with a chance of catching almost anything. Elephants and gummies are the most targeted species here. Big sharks are often hooked and lost and flathead to 4 kilos and mulloway to 10 kilos have been landed here in recent years. This is a low tide only location, so plan your trip accordingly.

Though I can't stress enough that this is a low tide only fishing location, don't be fooled by the colour of the "dry" sand along your walk. Short cuts are not always a good option and you could quickly find yourself up to your berries in mud. Follow the shoreline to the southern most point then around the north. Berley works well but it is most effective when fishing the last two hours of the ebb tide. Use a frozen berley log and put it into an onion bag. Toss this out on a long rope and let the tide disperse it. As the tide retreats, pick up the bag and toss it back out into the deeper water.

TENBY POINT

This area (Melway Ref 612 Q10) may not look like much of a fishing destination, but it sure does produce the goods, especially early in the season. Gummy sharks are the main target here with fish to 6 kilos more common than the big brutes. The good thing about this location is that it can provide the angler with numbers of fish.

Big snapper may be few and far between, but they do exist, and elephants will offer good sport during their season. This is a high tide hot spot that produces best after dark when big fish loose their inhibitions and move in to the shallows to feed.

The bottom is quote rocky and if you don't know exactly where to fish, you could be casting into a foot of water. The better location is to the left of the walkway. Once on the beach head east until you find the old pier ruins. Cast to the east of these on the high tide to the edge of the channel.

CORINELLA PIER

One of the best fish producing piers on Western Port along with the Warneet Pier, this structure (Melway Ref 612 Q10) situated on Peter Street, offers ample angling opportunity for those not fortunate enough to have access to a boat. For some reason, this structure attracts unusually large numbers of rock ling, trevally, gummies and mulloway. Rock ling is a magnificent eating fish and if I had to place my bets on where to catch one, this would be it.

It has good access to deep water in Corinella Channel and there are few other structures that see so many mulloway captures. Most of these fish are about the 2–4 kilo mark and take cut pilchard baits.

Fishing the flood tide on the lower landing is quite popular for those wanting to tangle with trevally. Throughout the summer months it is common to have large schools of trevally hold under the pier, a light berley trail will get them into a feeding frenzy.

Fishing the last hour of the flood tide and the first two hours of the ebb is the prime time to target and catch whiting. To the left of the pier, cast towards the barge landing but only 10 or so meters. A berley pot placed on the bottom next to the pier will bring them within casting range.

THE BLUFF (SETTLEMENT BLUFF)

Situated at the northern end of Coronet Bay, this popular location (Melway Ref 612 Q10) tapers down to allow land based action as well as boating protection from northerly winds. Whiting are a regular catch along with flathead, garfish, salmon, silvery trevally, mullet and squid. Land based angling opportunities are endless from this ledge. It is a low tide only location so to access the deeper water where you can expect to catch pinkie snapper to 40cm, silver trevally, elephants, gummy sharks, mulloway, whiting, flathead and salmon. Both paternoster rigs and running sinker rigs work well. A heavy strength leader ranging 30-60lb will be required as the area is very reefy.

BOAT RAMPS

LANG LANG

Don't bother. I would prefer not to fish than to use it again. Put in at Corinella and travel by water. This is what keeps people from fishing this area and in turn what makes the fishing so good.

GRANTVILLE

Don't bother. A single lane ramp in disrepair that is a long way from the water at low tide.

CORINELLA

Launching here is simple. A well protected ramp only 100 metres north of the pier (Melway Ref 612 Q10) allows launching and loading for craft up to 6 metres at all stages of the tide and bigger boats after about an hour of the flood. Follow the main road from the Bass Highway turn off and this road will lead you to the pier/ramp on Peter Street. It gets extremely busy here when the elephants are on, so be prepared for long waits of up to three hours.

It may be a long walk in and is not one for the faint hearted but Stockyard Point is well known for its gummy sharks, bronze whaler sharks and elephants. It is a low tide fishery only.

EAST ARM TO EASTERN ENTRANCE & OFFSHORE

Fishing the sand flats at San Remo is a productive location to flick soft plastics for flathead on low tide. Be very careful as the tide rushes in fast and you could get stranded.

EAST ARM TO EASTERN ENTRANCE

The more I fish south and north of the San Remo Bridge, the greater the appreciation I get for this part of the Port. Even though it is relatively small in area, it is extremely diverse. It is grossly underestimated by most anglers who only consider it as a passage to and from the ocean and not a serious fishing location in its own right. The tide rips through this area, therefore the shallower edges of the channel tend to be more productive. Squid, salmon, pike, flathead, whiting, trevally and small snapper are regular catches.

WHERE TO FISH

GRIFFITH POINT (FOOTS)

This is located on the mainland on the eastern headland of the Eastern Entrance. Here you will find whiting all year round along with salmon, pinkies, mullet, leatherjackets and good patches of big calamari. If you can find the whiting they will usually be in the 40–45 cm bracket and can be fished on both tides, with the flood preferred. Clean water will help to locate the sand holes in among the heavy, weedy bottom. Swell can be a problem, so care must be taken and you won't be able to fish here whenever you wish, due to weather.

BASKET BEACON (CLEELAND BIGHT)

This area is very popular with whiting and squid anglers and is located on the west side of the channel. This productive whiting ground produces on all tides with the ebb a little more productive. You will find plenty of broken ground here with short weed and lots of sand holes that vary in depth from 1.5–7 metres. This is excellent calamari ground from the start of September until the end of summer. Three prominent red buoys situated in Cleeland Bight are a good starting point for squid. Land based anglers can also have great success here. Anglers fishing from a kayak can launch with ease at Cleeland Bight. Located at the end of Cottosloe Ave at

Cape Woolamai, the carpark is practically on the beach. From there, you can work up and down the entrance covering some prime fishing real estate. A red channel marker to the east of these buoys is an excellent area for pinkies to 2.5 kilos from January to April.

SAN REMO BAR/REEF

Even though it is not given as much attention as other more popular areas, this location is very productive with quality whiting dominating. There are also some nice flathead and big calamari on the weed beds that start below the San Remo Pier before following the bar for about 500 metres. They then peter out into a series of sand channels and a small reef, which is seldom exposed. The tide moves quickly here, so fishing time is limited.

The reef itself holds big whiting, pinkies, salmon and calamari in its 2–5 metre surrounds. The last two hours of the ebb are most productive. During days where wind and swell is at its minimum strengths, drifting and casting soft plastics along the banks edge can see some good sized flathead caught.

NARROWS

This is the area where the water that is entering or exiting the Port with the tide moves under the San Remo Bridge. On either tide change, snapper can be caught by anchoring on the east side of the bridge. This area also produces salmon, the occasional mulloway and monster stingrays, so be prepared to get your arms stretched.

MAIN CHANNEL

The Main Channel runs from the San Remo Bridge and heads in a north-easterly direction for about 1.5 kilometres. This channel is well marked with both port and starboard markers, but because of the strength of the tide, care must be taken. On arrival at the top of the channel—indicated by a 10 second flashing red light—you will be able to fish this area for a large variety of fish.

It is a very popular area for local anglers who catch good numbers

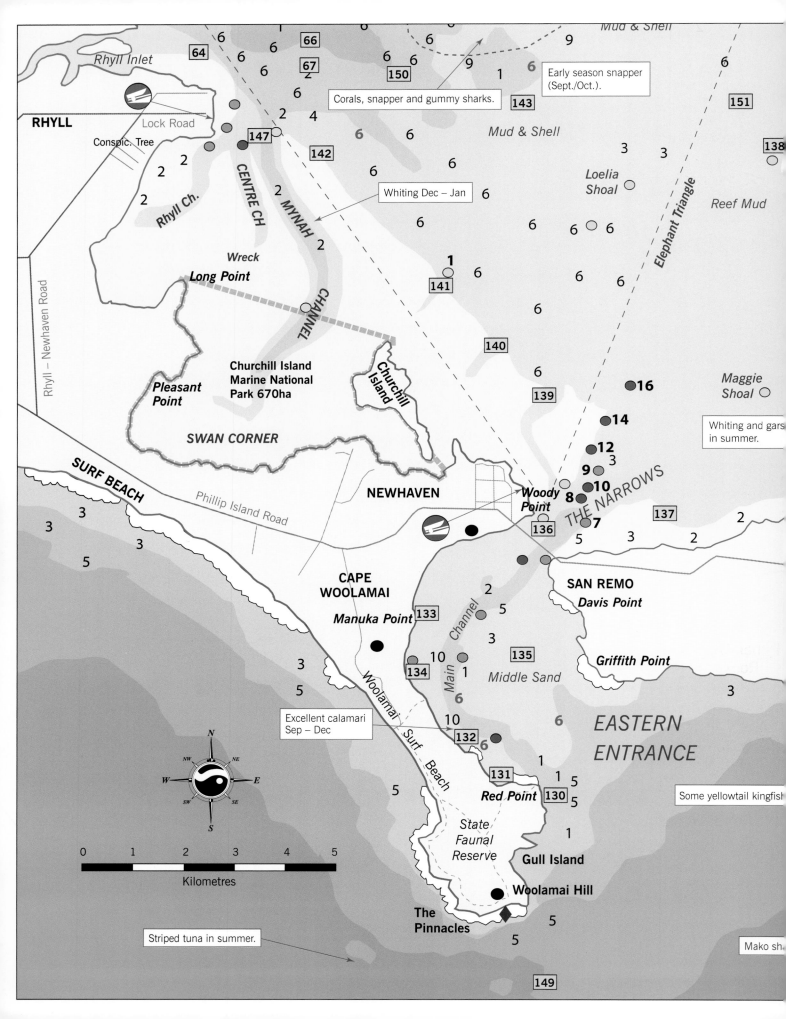

RHYLL

Rhyll Inlet

Lock Road

Conspic. Tree

64

66

67

150

6 6 6 6 66

6 6 9

6 6 9 1

2 6 6 820

6 6

143

151

Early season snapper (Sept./Oct.).

Corals, snapper and gummy sharks.

Mud & Shell

147

142

2 2 2 2 4

2 2

2

Rhyll Ch.

CENTRE CH

MYNAH

CHANNEL

Whiting Dec – Jan

6 6

6 6

6

6 6

6 6 6

3 3

138

Loelia Shoal

Reef Mud

Elephant Triangle

Wreck

Long Point

Pleasant Point

Churchill Island
Marine National
Park 670ha

Churchill Island

SWAN CORNER

1

141

6

6 6

140

6

139

6

16

14

12

9

10

8

7

3

Maggie Shoal

Whiting and gars in summer.

THE NARROWS

137

SURF BEACH

3

3

3

5

Phillip Island Road

NEWHAVEN

Woody Point

136

5

3

2

2

CAPE WOOLAMAI

Manuka Point

133

Channel

Main

2

5

3

135

Middle Sand

SAN REMO

Davis Point

Griffith Point

3

2

3

Woolamai

3

5

10

134

1

10

Surf Beach

Excellent calamari
Sep – Dec

132

6

131

130

Red Point

6

6

6

EASTERN ENTRANCE

Some yellowtail kingfish

1 1 5

1 5

1

State Faunal Reserve

Gull Island

Woolamai Hill

5

5

N
NW NE
W   E
SW SE
S

0 1 2 3 4 5
Kilometres

The Pinnacles

Striped tuna in summer.

Mako sh.

149

Rhyll – Newhaven Road

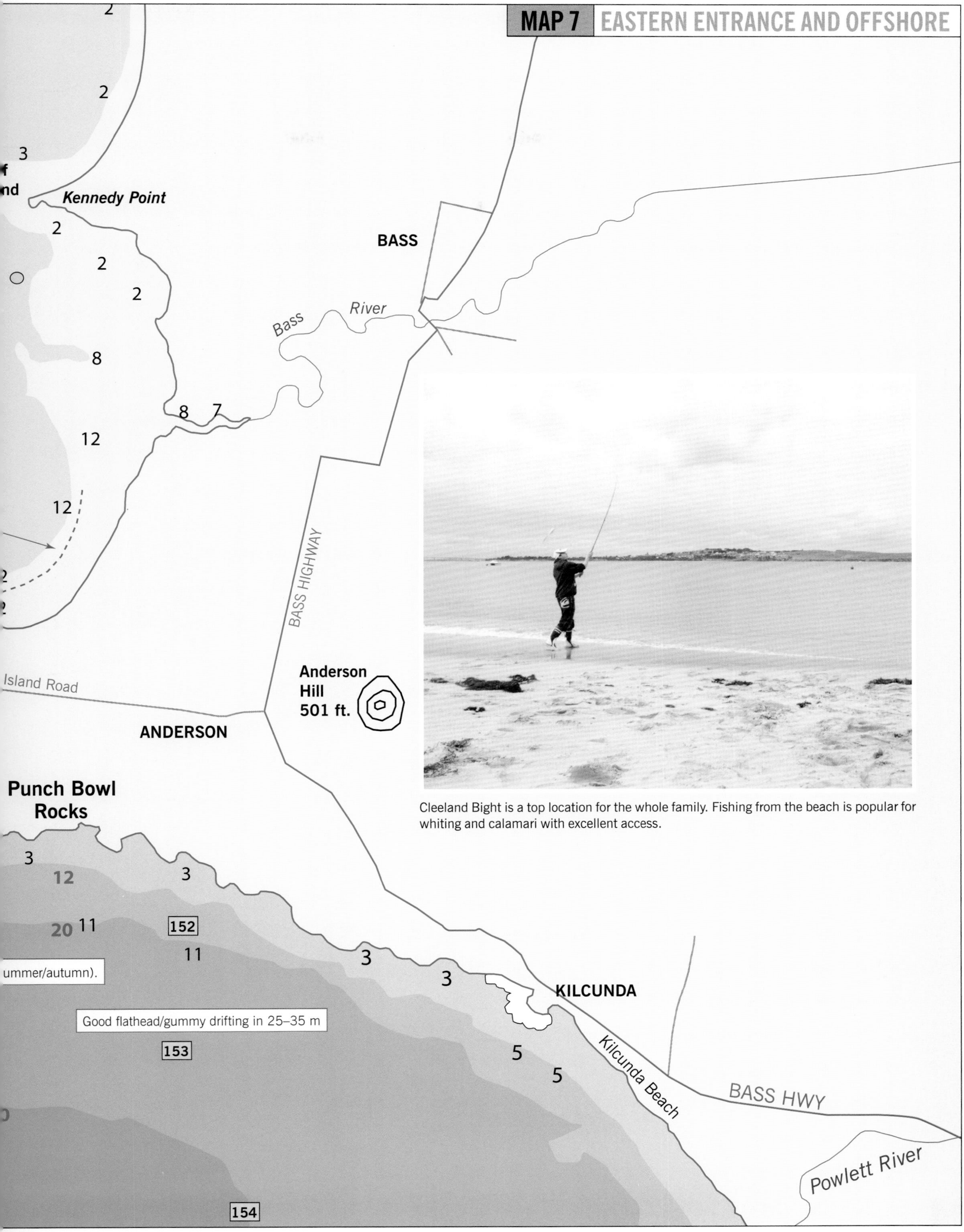

MAP 7 EASTERN ENTRANCE AND OFFSHORE

2

2

3

Kennedy Point

BASS

2

2

2

Bass   River

8

8   7

12

12

Island Road

BASS HIGHWAY

**Anderson
Hill
501 ft.**

ANDERSON

Cleeland Bight is a top location for the whole family. Fishing from the beach is popular for whiting and calamari with excellent access.

**Punch Bowl
Rocks**

3

12   3

20 11   152

11

ummer/autumn).

Good flathead/gummy drifting in 25–35 m

153

3

3

3   **KILCUNDA**

5

5

Kilcunda Beach

BASS HWY

Powlett River

154

GPS MARKS FOR MAP 7 EASTERN ENTRANCE & OFFSHORE

130: OLD WOOLAMAI QUARRY
(LANDMARK & NAVIGATIONAL HAZARD)
S 38 32 425 E 145 20 682

131: COLIN GUILMARTIN BASKET BEACON TO CLEELAND BIGHT
(SQUID, PINKIES, WHITING, SALMON, MULLET, GENERAL AREA
RANGING 1.5–7 METRES)
S 38 32 426 E 145 20 892

132: COLIN GUILMARTIN BASKET BEACON TO CLEELAND BIGHT
S 38 32 426 E 145 20 666

133: COLIN GUILMARTIN BASKET BEACON TO CLEELAND BIGHT
S 38 31 796 E 145 20 666

134: COLIN GUILMARTIN BASKET BEACON TO CLEELAND BIGHT
S 38 31 847 E 145 20 909

135: COLIN GUILMARTIN SAN REMO REEF
(MIXED BAG, LAST OF EBB)
S 38 32 010 E 145 21 349

136: MIDDLE OF SAN REMO BRIDGE
S 38 31 124 E 145 21 873

137: COLIN GUILMARTIN DICKIES BAY
(WHITING, GARS, SALMON, GENERAL AREA)
S 38 30 735 E 145 23 550

138: COLIN GUILMARTIN REEF ISLAND
(WHITING, WEST OF ISLAND, SPRING TO LATE JUNE)
S 38 28 250 E 145 23 910

139: COLIN GUILMARTIN THE GRAVEL
(WHITING, PINKIES, FAST FLOW, BOTH TIDES)
S 38 30 198 E 145 22 607

140: NEW HAVEN GUTTER EXIT (NAVIGATION HAZARD)
S 38 30 102 E 145 21 994

141: COLIN GUILMARTIN ENTRANCE TO BOYS HOME CHANNEL
(SERIOUS NAVIGATION HAZARD)
S 38 29 740 E 145 21 340

142: PENINSULA AND WESTERN PORT CHARTERS RHYLL
(WHITING, APPROX. 6.5 METRES, NOV–MARCH)
S 38 28 077 E 145 20 197

143: PENINSULA AND WESTERN PORT CHARTERS LOELIA SHOAL
(ELEPHANTS, APPROX. 4.5 METRES, MARCH–APRIL)
S 38 27 961 E 145 22 113

147: RHYLL CLOSE (ELEPHANT FISH)
S 38 27 593 E 145 18 952

149: WOOLAMAI OFFSHORE (MAKOS AND BLUES)
S 38 36 036 E 145 21 085

150: CORAL (SNAPPER AND WHITING)
S 38 26 779 E 145 19 796

151: MUDSHELL (MULLOWAY)
S 38 27 529 E 145 22 784

152: KILCUNDA OFFSHORE (THRESHER SHARKS)
S 38 33 483 E 145 27 242

153: KILCUNDA OFFSHORE (REEF SNAPPER)
S 38 35 059 E 145 25 250

154: WOOLAMAI KINK
(MAKOS, BLUES, THRESHERS)
S 38 38 287 E 145 21 734

Cleeland Bight opens up into Bass Stait and gets a regular flush of clean ocean water. It is a top fishing location both land based and from the boat.

Looking towards Dickies Bay from Newhaven at low tide, you can clearly see that fishing the edge of the channel is mandatory. These areas are very productive for whiting in the summer months.

of quality whiting up to 600 grams, trevally and elephants on the channel edges.

Whilst fishing for whiting, it is also a good idea to fish for snapper or gummy sharks when the tide slackens. Simply cast your snapper bait well back and clear of the whiting rods, thus avoiding the possibility of tangles.

Some big snapper roam in the deep water at the head of this channel, but due to the heavy tidal influence there is only a small window of opportunity for anglers who target them. Big gummies are also caught with regularity in this area. Most anglers enjoy success while fishing at night as the sharks move out of the deep and on to the shallow banks to feed on crustaceans such as crabs.

Newhaven Gutter (Stevie's Hole)

This small gutter runs from the Newhaven Pier past the boat ramp and follows the island shoreline towards Rhyll for 1 kilometre before emptying into the Main Channel. This gutter is marked on both sides and is only 100 metres from shore. Small and large whiting are taken in this little channel for most of the season and good schools of gars make it their home at various times over the spring/summer period, especially toward the mouth. A new launching facility was built in the late 1990s and is far more suitable for bigger craft than the old, flat ramp. This has made for much better access to Bass Strait through Western Port's East Entrance for the growing band of mako, blue and thresher shark fishos.

If you exit the gutter and turn either left or right, follow the bank to find some good school whiting grounds. Try fishing in 3 metres or less of water as the tide starts to flood. Move small distances as often as you need to in order to find the fish. Berley is essential.

Boys Home Channel

This small channel is a serious navigation hazard so care must be taken at all times and be careful when locating this mark. It is often confused with the Newhaven Gutter and was named after the old Newhaven boy's home, which it runs towards. This can be a dynamite whiting spot at times with the ebb tide producing best results.

Green Triangle

About 200 metres north of the bridge on the San Remo side you will find a small pole with a green triangle on it. Work your way east from this marker on the last two hours of the flood tide. There is a very prominent sandy channel here, which runs all the way to Dickies Bay. This area produces plenty of whiting, salmon, trevally and the occasional snapper. The tidal flow is very fast here and berley is a must if you are looking for quantities of fish. Try fishing this area on the start of the ebb before the tide picks up too much momentum.

Dickies Bay

Found just behind the San Remo Police Station in a north-easterly direction from the San Remo Bridge is Dickies Bay. This is not a bay as such, but at low tide a definite bay that has been carved out of the exposed mud banks is visible. The bottom here changes from sand to light rubble and weed to mud. This area holds good numbers of whiting year round and fishes well throughout the winter when most other areas are quiet. This shallow bank responds well to berley as it draws the fish to you instead of having to go to them. Toadies can be a problem, so you may have to relocate if they move in. This area also produces garfish, salmon, trevally and mullet.

Many locals head for Dickies Bay and few return without a good catch of whiting. From September through to December, garfish are plentiful. A surface berley trail will bring them within casting range. A float setup is effective around two hours either side of a tide change. As the tide increases its strength, free float a paternoster rig with small size 12 long shank hooks down the trail with no sinker weight. Garfish are partial to a wide range of baits but maggots, dough and silverfish work best.

The Corals is one of the most well known fishing GPS marks in the Port. Those that fish it have regular success on mulloway, gummy sharks, snapper and elephants in season.

ANDERSON'S PEG (MAGGIE SHOAL)

This area is a navigation hazard at low tide so care must be taken if approaching this mark. It is a very well known local mark that produces whiting and garfish throughout the summer months. The bottom around the Peg is made up of broken ground ranging 2–5 metres with an extensive fishing area north to Reef Island and east to the Bass River.

A slow moving tide here allows fishing all day, with berley very effective. On the ebb tide a careful eye will be needed to keep your craft away from these broken or reefy grounds. This area is exposed to north and westerly winds.

Calamari are also a popular target, especially over the weed beds. While at anchor, set a berley trail and fish silver whiting on squid jags and suspend them under floats for best results.

BASS RIVER

The entrance area to the Bass River is a popular mark for local anglers leaving from the Newhaven Ramp. This spot has a slowly sloping bank consisting of broken ground, sand and grass patches and offers a big area of fishing for the whiting that remain here all season. Leatherjackets, mullet and grass whiting also make a good variety of fish for the bag.

The mouth of the river also produces some quality garfish and squid fishing with the occasional estuary perch to 2.3 kilos taken literally by mistake while fishing for flathead.

The river itself holds fair populations of black bream, estuary perch, mullet, salmon, flathead and the occasional mulloway.

To be successful, you have to nut out the tides and fish them to the best of your ability. Kayak access is great from the end of Bass Landing Road where you can easily slide in off the bank. There is also an old boat ramp but a 4WD is required and tinny's no longer than 4 meters should be launched. Bream and Perch favour soft plastic and hard body lures flicked to the edges of the mangroves on high tide.

THE WRECK

The wreck, which lies 1 kilometre in a southerly direction from the Rhyll Pier, is one of the most prominent marks from Rhyll. This wreck is the remains of the steam tug Minah, which served under the Geelong Harbour Trust until the end of World War II. Under private ownership it broke its moorings at Rhyll in a northerly gale and was battered and eventually came to rest at its present position.

Although the wreck lies in the mud, a channel runs past on the eastern side and whiting and flathead are taken along this channel at any stage of the tide. The channel continues past Churchill Island and heads in a westerly direction before emptying out in Swan Corner, very close to Phillip Island.

As this is the only channel between Churchill Island and the wreck, care will need to be taken or you will finish up on the mud. You are surrounded here by kilometres of mud so if you land yourself on a bank, you could spend the rest of the day waiting for water to float your boat again.

THE ELEPHANT TRIANGLE

I first came up with this imaginary triangle while writing an article for a national magazine over a decade ago. When I was looking at the areas where 90 per cent of elephant captures took place, I noticed that they fell very neatly into a triangle that I drew over my map of the Port. It starts at Corinella and goes in a straight line across to Tortoise Head and then down to Newhaven before heading back to Corinella.

If you draw this you will notice that it forms an almost perfect equilateral triangle that covers the best elephant grounds in the Port. If you want to find the elephants of Western Port, then this is the place to start. The Elephant Triangle is now one of the most fished areas on the Port. Elephants are in their prime from February through May. Fish the moon phases in this area for best results.

THE NITTS

This mark has come from obscurity in recent years due to up to date reports from the Kilcunda Caravan Park. It as a very productive area for small pinkies in the 40 cm and below bracket from January through to March. Early in the season it is not uncommon for bigger snapper to school up in this area, with large school shark a big possibility in the warmer summer months. Some big gummies will also turn up at this time. The bottom here is heavy and rough, so you will have to be prepared to loose a bit of tackle. It is always worth putting a pipi out here as the tide slackens, for the occasional whiting to over 50 centimetres.

THE CORALS AREA

Some amazing fishing has taken place on the Corals over the past five years. Bag limit snapper catches are just out of control with up to 40 snapper to 20 pounds taken in just a couple of hours fishing. This spot fires really well early in the season and through to Christmas, but it is always worth a look.

It is not an 'X marks the spot' situation, with the Corals more of a general area. Depths will range from 5–20 metres depending on your exact location.

Fish tend to graze in this area and move through every 20–30 minutes. Berley is a good way of holding them in the zone and be sure to watch the movements of other boats as this will give you an excellent indication as to where the fish are. It is not uncommon to see a couple of hundred boats fishing here on a nice day.

The bottom is made up of gravel and cunje and a stony grey coral-like substance, hence the name.

The area also produces gummies, schoolies, mulloway and rock ling. You can always find somewhere to fish here regardless of the tide and I have had some of my best Western Port snapper sessions on this mark.

There are also some very nice sized flathead to be caught as well. Drifting is the preferred method and allows you to cover ground to find where they are holding.

FISHING OFFSHORE

GULL ISLAND

If you take a good look at the map you will notice a small island between Red Point and Cape Woolamai. This stretch of water, including the island itself, holds a vast number of species that respond well to baits and lures. Barracouta, trevally, big salmon, pike, snook, scad, kingfish and a host of other species all call this area home.

It is extremely well protected from westerly winds and offers beautiful scenery with steep cliffs dropping into the ocean. Just motor along casting soft plastics and metal lures in towards the rocks.

There are some nice pinnacles out on the point of the Cape that produce big salmon and some kingfish in summer.
You can also anchor up about 100 metres from the rocks and fish for gummies, snapper and threshers.

EASTERN ENTRANCE TO BLACK HEAD

This covers a fair amount of water that in my opinion receives little to no attention from amateur anglers. This is especially true the further east you push.

You really can try anything here. Trolling close to the rocks will produce salmon, kingfish, couta, snook, pike and even a thresher shark if you are prepared to put out a big lure.

If you want to bait fish, then the world, or should I say Strait, is your oyster. There are isolated inshore reefs stretched right along the coast that hold species ranging from snapper to big whiting. If you can find the edge of the reef you will also encounter gummy sharks. Make sure you have some serious gear on board as threshers and seven gills often take bottom baits intended for much smaller fish — or they take the fish after you've hooked it. Now that's a fun experience!

Drift fishing with a paternoster rig is highly effective for flathead. Sand, blue spot and tiger varieties are available and can fetch a fair size. Silver whiting are also a common catch for those fishing with size 10 long shank hooks. They are in plaque proportions during the summer months and very few people actually target them. Due to the strength of the offshore current, substantial lead will be required to keep your baits within reach of the bottom. Try to use as little as possible but if your bait isn't on the bottom, catching quality fish will become a challenge.

SHARKS

There is plenty of room for the serious offshore angler here too with makos, blues, whalers, threshers and the occasional white sniffing around.

Threshers tend to hang around in 20–35 metres of water over reef or broken ground, therefore this is the best place to target them.
If you are looking for the big boys head offshore between the 40 and 70 metre line from December through to April. Makos will tend to be found around the 40 metre mark, plus the 60–70 metre line is your best chance of locking horns with a blue. Once you start to berley, you can't choose what will come up the trail, so good luck.

This area holds some of the best shark fishing you may ever encounter. A world record 86.4 kilo thresher was taken here by Russell Taylor on 6 kilo line in December 1997 and in January 1994 I landed a AAA Australian Record mako of 275 kilos off Woolamai. Fortunately threshers average 15–30 kilos and makos 20–50 kilos, so you might not need a bigger boat yet!

For more information on sharks refer to earlier chapters, Sharks within the Port and Sharks Offshore.

TUNA

Not a common topic of conversation these days, Tuna were quite a common catch back in the 1970's where striped tuna turned up annually. The commercial fishing fleet from San Remo would head out in season and net schools for local markets. Years passed and the tuna never returned until 2010 when huge of schools tuna swarmed offshore from Phillip Island. February through to April is the prime time to target them.

Trolling is the best technique with small 4" white coloured squid skirts and 4" jerk bait soft plastics the top lures.

When searching for tuna, pick the weather and head offshore. Watch the birds for diving activity and head over to investigate. If you notice any surface commotion, troll around the area for success.

Mako sharks are certainly the Apex predator of Bass Strait and are highly prized. Offering a wide range of sport fishing techniques, they are a lot of fun to catch.

Punchbowl Rocks is a very dangerous fishing location and many anglers have lost their lives fishing from the platform. It is not recommended to fish despite the fish that can be caught.

Boat ramp locations

Newhaven

With no ramp on the mainland at San Remo, the Newhaven Ramp is the closest available (Melway Ref 632 J7). Only 100 metres across the bridge turn right and follow the road for 500 metres and you will arrive at the Newhaven Pier. It is a two lane ramp with sealed parking and fish cleaning facilities. This relatively new facility, which was upgraded in 1999, is suitable for most trailer boats on all tides. However, a very low tide can cause some grief, so it will be best to be patient in this situation.

Rhyll

The Rhyll ramp is located alongside the pier. It is a dual lane all weather, all tide ramp that will take boats to 6 metres plus. Follow the main Cowes Road from the San Remo Bridge until arriving at the Rhyll turn-off on the right. This road then leads directly to the pier (Melway Ref 632 E3). There is ample sealed parking.

Shore Based Fishing

Cleeland Bight

This sandy beach (Melway Ref 634 D11) offers land based anglers the chance to battle monster calamari and flathead with salmon, whiting and leatherjackets also available. It is situated near the old Woolamai boat ramp on Phillip Island. Best time of year for the calamari is September to late November with summer and spring good for all other species.

From the carpark, fish right in front of the two red buoy's situated around 80 meters out from the shore. Cast towards these with a squid jag under a float for best results and let the current carry float over the weed beds. Walking south towards the entrance a large

sand dune is noticeable. Casting out into the entrance from beneath the dune is productive for whiting and pinkie snapper.

San Remo Pier

You will always get a fresh feed of fish if you go to the San Remo pier (Melway Ref 634 H7). There is a great fish and chip shop just a stone's throw away! The tide races past this structure, which can make fishing difficult at times.

Whiting, pike, barracouta, flathead and monster stingrays call this area home. It is not one of my favourite piers, but it can produce the goods from time to time. Fishing an hour either side of the high tide change is effective for calamari, particularly at night. Silver whiting is the most popular bait to use.

Newhaven Pier

You will see this structure on you right as you drive over the bridge onto Phillip Island (Melway Ref 634 H6).

Plenty of silver trevally, mullet, and salmon are taken from this pier on both tides. Elephants and pinkies to 2 kilos are also taken here. The best times are the last hour of the ebb and the first two hours of the flood. Whitebait, pillies and pipis are used with success. King George whiting do frequent this area with monsters taken occasionally.

A berley pot suspended along side of the pylons at either end of the pier works well. You will need substantial weight placed into the pot to prevent the currents pressure pushing it to the surface.

Rhyll Pier

Quite a variety of fish are taken from this solid structure (Melway Ref 632 E3) on Beach Road Rhyll. Flathead, silver trevally, whiting, mullet and leatherjackets are caught during the season, making a trip down worthwhile. Elephants will also turn up here when they are in the Port in force.

Because the area is mostly shallow with a mud substrate bottom, flathead are also a common catch. Blue bait threaded onto a paternoster rig works well.

Red Point

The rocky outcrop at Red Point is a prime location (Melway Ref 633 G1) for larger snapper from the shore, but the long walk into this spot deters most anglers. It is about a 4 kilometre walk from where you park your vehicle a few hundred metres past the Woolamai General Store. A little berley will also attract salmon, sweep, calamari, mullet and the occasional whiting. A running float rig tends to be most effective, as bottom rigs are prone to snags. Casting 60g metal slugs into the entrance will see pike, snook and barracouta catch. Kingfish are also a possible target from February until April. This area fishes well on an evening high tide.

Punch Bowl Rocks

I am almost reluctant to mention this spot, which is located at the end of Punch Bowl Road (Melway Ref 627 J9), a road leading to the right about 4 kilometres back toward the Bass Highway from San Remo. Not only is the access track extremely dangerous down to the rock platform, so too is the rock platform itself, which is only a metre or so out of the water at high tide.

Large salmon, big snapper, trevally, yellowtail kingfish, gummy sharks, barracouta and mullet are regularly caught in the deep water here from November to March. Some land based game fishing for sharks such as threshers and bronzies also takes place here.

Although this is a much talked about spot by local anglers, I would not recommend negotiating the track if it's wet following rain or if you are not fit, agile and sure footed. This is certainly no area to take children fishing.

If you do intend to fish the area wear an inflatable approved life vest such as a Stormy Seas and never ever fish alone. If in doubt, don't go out. No fish is worth a life.

PHILLIP ISLAND LAND BASED

The only thing stopping any angler from some action packed fishing on Phillip Island is his or her imagination. With over 25 kilometres of coastline between San Remo and the Nobbies, you are sure to find a nice spot to cast a line. Whether it's a rock platform, a sheltered bay or a pristine surf beach, you are bound to find a host of species ready and willing to thrill.

Always keep in mind that some of the locations mentioned can be dangerous and slippery most of the time. Always take care and never turn your back on the ocean.

WHERE TO FISH

WOOLAMAI SURF BEACH

This area is one of the most famous surf beaches in the State and definitely the most popular on the island (Melway Ref 634 D12). Access is easy, after crossing the San Remo Bridge on to the Island, just turn left into Cape Woolamai Rd and make your way towards the beach. There are actually two carparks in which you can park at. The first is Anzacs Beach which provides access to two deep gutters, one to the east and the other the west. The Western gutter is quite reefy and it is very common to catch silver trevally and pinkie snapper from in the warmer months. The eastern gutter is particularly productive for big salmon throughout winter.

A large stretch of clean, deep surf gives plenty of fishing space. Australian salmon are the main quarry, with fish to 3 kilos taken at times. Most fish are about 500 gram to 1.5 kilo and it is possible to find them in numbers if you berley. Blue bait, whitebait, pipis and surf poppers are all popular with the salmon. Yellow eye mullet and the odd gummy shark are also taken all along the beach with the last two hours of the flood and the first two hours of the ebb normally the most productive.

This beach is very popular with surfers and swimmers, so please respect their space.

SMITHS BEACH

If you travel about 15 kilometres west from Woolamai you will come across Smiths Beach (Melway Ref 632 A7). This is also a popular beach for surf and rock fishing.

This area can get extremely busy around school holidays so be prepared to get up early or to share the beach with swimmers and sunbakers. Salmon, flathead and mullet are caught from the beach during the day with the chance of a nice gummy shark after dark. There are some rocks nearby that will produce a whole variety of fish if berley is added to the area. Whiting, sweep, garfish, leatherjackets and salmon are all a possibility.

KITTY MILLER BAY

This is a hidden gem on Philip Island that sees some hot fishing from time to time. Kitty Miller Bay (Melway Ref 631 E7) can be found at the end of Kitty Miller Bay Rd and does not receive the same attention as other land based locations.

A long cast on a low tide will find some nice sand patches with occasional whiting to 950 grams and trevally to 2 kilos. Good garfish can also be berleyed up to the rocks. Quality fish like these make a trip to the area well worthwhile. Take a look for yourself and you won't be disappointed.

CAT BAY

Cat Bay is more known as a surf beach rather than a fishing beach.

THE NOBBIES

The best area to fish around the Nobbies is at the small rocky outcrop called Cowrie Beach (Melway Ref 631 B7). These rocks are located to the right hand side of the road, about 800 metres short of the Nobbies Seal Observatory Car Park. This area can only be fished to two hours either side of the low tide as swells flood over the rocks on the high. A light northerly wind offers the perfect angling scenario as it flattens the swell. Berley is the key to success here.

Big leatherjackets, garfish, zebra fish and salmon are the prime species to target, but you will have to work your way through the wrasse.

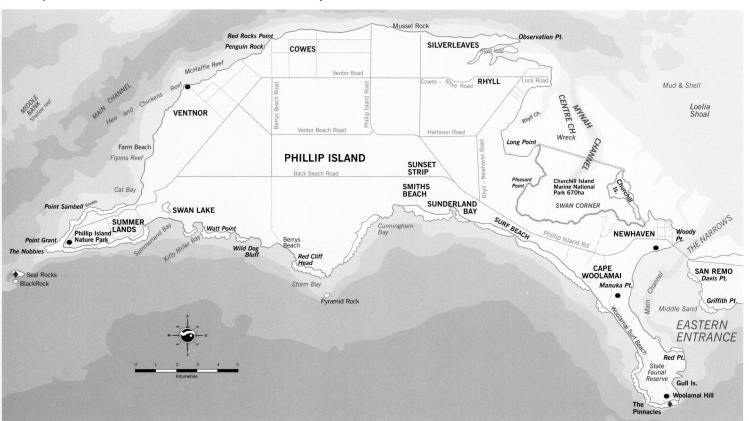

KILCUNDA TO CAPE PATERSON

n the middle of winter when the rest of the fishing world slows close to a standstill, it is this stretch of coastline between Kilcunda and Cape Patterson that keeps the fishing world spinning. Between late May and mid August the species that inhabit this area come out in force and the seasonal species such as salmon move in for a good feed. This beach and rocky coast boasts a variety of good surf fishing and rock fishing locations and is extremely popular as a venue for surf fishing competitions with angling clubs from around the State. In the winter months, thousands of anglers from all over Melbourne make their way down to the Bass beaches in search of big salmon and yellow eye mullet.

Kilcunda is a cute little township about 8 kilometres down the Bass Highway, from the Phillip Island roundabout. Opposite the Kilcunda Hotel is the Kilcunda Caravan Park, which is owned and operated by my good friends Colin and Stevie Guilmartin. This beautiful caravan park (03 5678 7260) overlooks Bass Strait and has great views down the coast towards Cape Paterson. Colin is a keen angler and is always happy to hear about your catch or to give some advice to keen anglers. There are some rocks at the base of the park that regularly see catches of nice whiting, leatherjackets and salmon.

KILCUNDA SURF BEACH

This beach is well marked and is situated just past the town itself heading towards Wonthaggi (Melway Ref 612 Q11). Cemetery beach is very popular with anglers and is named after the cemetery that you park next to in order to get beach access. Both beaches offer good fishing for salmon and mullet with flathead, trevally and barracouta a pleasant by-catch. The rocky outcrop in front of the trestle bridge is very productive for a wide range of species including salmon, trevally, pinkie snapper, leatherjacket, mullet, flathead, wrasse and gummy sharks. Fishing from the rocks can be dangerous, always watch the ocean swells.

Either tide change is fishable for these species but I do prefer an hour or two before and after the high. Gummies can be taken from the beach at night along with seven gill sharks and threshers with the full moon cycle most productive. Even snapper to 7 kilos have been taken here in September, but this is a rare occurrence. Even rarer, kingfish have been a reported capture in the summer months for those willing to put in the effort. These have been caught while fishing for gummy sharks during the day.

WILLIAMSON'S BEACH

This beach can be found by turning right into Lower Powlett Rd just as you approach the town of Wonthaggi. The surf here offers similar fishing to Kilcunda but generally fishes better than other beaches in the area. Because it is off the beaten track it receives less pressure so there are more fish for fewer anglers to share, it is also one of the deepest beaches along this stretch of coast. If you're after big salmon, this is the beach to be trying your luck.

Berley works extremely well; tuna oil infused pellets are a godsend.

POWLETT RIVER

The Powlett River turn off is situated about 2 kilometres south east of Kilcunda (Melway Ref 612 R12). Follow this road for another 2 kilometres and you will arrive at the car park, which is only a short walk to the surf and river mouth.

On the surf, salmon and yellow eye mullet are taken in good numbers, with gummy and school shark being popular on evening and during the night. This area fishes well after good rain when the river is open to the sea. You may have to walk down the beach to avoid the dirty water, but find the tide line between the two and anything could happen.

The Powlett River estuary hold some great fish even though it is quite small and receives a lot of angling pressure form amateurs and illegal netters. Mullet are taken in good numbers, whilst further up the estuary, black bream and estuary perch to 1.5 kilos are attainable. Bait, lure and fly techniques all work well. There is a good hole on the bend about 100 metres from the beach that produces monster bream and some mulloway on bait.

Williamson's Beach

This beach can be found by turning right into Lower Powlett Rd just as you approach the town of Wonthaggi. The surf here offers similar fishing to Kilcunda but generally fishes better than other beaches in the area. Because it is off the beaten track it receives less pressure so there are more fish for fewer anglers to share.

There are usually some deep holes on this beach not too far from the car park. It is worth asking your local tackle store or checking up to date reports before heading to any of these Bass beaches.

WRECK BEACH AND HARMERS HAVEN

If you follow the Cape Patterson Rd from the township of Wonthaggi signs will appear on your right that will lead you to Wreck Beach (Melway Ref 612 R12). Follow this road all the way to the beach where both surf and rock fishing options will present themselves. The beach offers similar results to the Bass beaches, with salmon the main fare.

Harmers Haven is adjacent to Wreck Beach and is a great place to find big seven gill sharks from the shore. Sweep, mullet, leatherjackets and wrasse are all caught from this platform.

CAPE PATTERSON

About 8 kilometres from Wonthaggi is the small town of Cape Patterson. This area is popular with holidaymakers as it offers fishing in many different forms including rock, surf and boat.

There is a reef in front of the Surf Life Saving Club that fishes well on the ebb tide for a wide range of species. Salmon, barracouta, flathead and trevally can all be caught from the beach with boaties occasionally stumbling across some nice patches of whiting.

If you follow the shoreline west for about a kilometre you will come upon an area known as Second Surf. Here, boaties will find whiting and pinkies with schools of barracouta often moving through. Salmon, mullet and garfish are taken from the shore on a paternoster rig baited with cut pilchard, blue bait, pipis and squid.

Good luck on your next Western Port adventure, and remember that the best time to catch a fish is within ten minutes of catching a fish.

In saying that, the good thing about Western Port is that you can always find a fish somewhere, and you can always find somewhere to fish.

Yours in fishing
Paul Worsteling

BOAT - CAR - DOOR MAT

HELM MATS

700mm

Non-slip base

20mm

www.afntv.com.au

The **AFN Deluxe Helm Mat** will make a great addition to your boat. Made out of long lasting neoprene and 20mm thickness will add that little bit of extra comfort on-board. With a non-slip base to ensure you won't be taking a dive into the water!

The Helm Mat measures 700mm x 400mm (Area: 0.28m2), perfect for wiping those deck boots on.

Helm mats are a hard wearing, soft and cushion deck for all helmsman stations in small to large craft.

Make long hours behind the wheel comfortable!.

With a range of cool retro designs on offer, you will be happy to welcome your mates on-board.

Brown Trout	AC7432	Marlin	AC7333	White Pointer	AC7357	Flathead

  (Marlin)  (White Pointer)  (Flathead)

Snapper	AC7319	Squid	AC7047	Barramundi	AC7326	Bream

Murray Cod	AC7340	Mangrove Jack	AC8170	Tuna	AC8200	Spanish Mackerel

Available from your local tackle/outdoors
store or call (03) 9729 8788 for stockists!

www.afn.com.au

 AFN